the day i c

# the day i died

remarkable true stories of
near-death experience

T A M M Y    C O H E N

JOHN BLAKE

Published by John Blake Publishing Ltd,
3 Bramber Court, 2 Bramber Road,
London W14 9PB, England

www.blake.co.uk

First published in paperback in 2006

ISBN 1 84454 249 1

British Library Cataloguing-in-Publication Data:

A catalogue record for this book is available from the British Library.

Design by www.envydesign.co.uk

Printed in Great Britain by Creative Print and Design, Wales

3 5 7 9 10 8 6 4 2

Papers used by John Blake Publishing are natural, recyclable products made from wood grown in sustainable forests. The manufacturing processes conform to the environmental regulations of the country of origin.

Every attempt has been made to contact the relevant copyright-holders, but some were unobtainable. We would be grateful if the appropriate people could contact us.

Every case history in this book is included with the consent of those involved. Names have been changed where requested.

Information contained in this guide is for the purpose of informing the reader of the publications and sources available to people who wish to investigate near-death experiences. The publisher shall not be held responsible for any advice or information provided by these third parties.

To Otis, Jake and Billie

# PROLOGUE

I'LL ADMIT IT. I wasn't completely buying this whole Near-Death Experience thing. When the idea of this book was first mentioned, I wasn't exactly shouting my joy from the rooftops.

Yes, I knew there were people who claimed to have had a glimpse through the net curtain of death into what lies beyond, but I was sure there had to be some other explanation. They were bonkers. They were religious zealots. They were hallucinating. Trauma had caused their brains to go into some sort of chemical meltdown that brought on delusions.

There were a hundred different reasons why people might be coming up with stories of how they 'died' and came back again. I entertained them all. All except one — that what they were describing might actually have happened.

I'm a natural sceptic. I don't have an inbuilt religious or spiritual framework on which something like NDE would naturally hang. Where is the proof of NDE? I wanted to know. Where is the scientific evidence for it?

Well, after spending months researching the subject and talking to hundreds of people, I know that, while there is a steadily growing body of scientific research into NDE, actual proof continues to be elusive. What does exist irrefutably, however, is a colossal collection of anecdotal evidence from 'experiencers' themselves and from those who've witnessed their experiences, in which the points of similarity are undeniably strong and yet for which there exists no common set of circumstances to provide a ready explanation for these similarities.

For me, the first surprise came early on. While talking to friends and colleagues about the subject of my latest research (accompanied, on my part, I must say by plenty of eye rolling and brow raising) I was amazed to find people I'd known for years commenting breezily, 'Oh yes, that happened to me.'

Suddenly, what had seemed like a bizarre phenomenon, something which existed on the fringes of 'normal' society — like Bigfoot sightings or alien abductions — was turning out to be as mainstream as chocolate digestives and *Who Wants to be a Millionaire*.

Strangest of all was when Michael, my own partner of fifteen years, admitted that, would you believe it, he'd had his own near-death experience after an allergic reaction to anaesthetic during an operation to reset a broken wrist when he was still in his teens. While he couldn't recall enough of the details to make it into this book, it was an eye-opening discovery.

All over the world, in every office you work in, every street you visit, there are people going about their everyday business, utterly convinced that they've had a glimpse into the twilight zone – into the dimension that is outside of life, and yet not 'death' either, at least not as we know it. These aren't extremists, or religious fundamentalists. Nor have they lost touch with reality. They are ordinary people to whom an extraordinary thing has happened.

That, for me, has been the great revelation of this book. That the exceptional exists all around us, and within us – and that, in this world where advertising is everything, the truly remarkable can pass uncelebrated, untrumpeted, like an unclaimed Lottery prize.

The people in this book gave up their time generously and without any hope of reward beyond an opportunity to expand general awareness of the experience they all share.

Let's hope they're not disappointed.

# ACKNOWLEDGEMENTS

I'd like to thank the following people:

Wensley Clarkson for his encouragement and blind faith.

Dr Peter Fenwick, Dr Jeffrey Long, Kenneth Williams, Linda Stewart, Ornella Corazza, Anne Eastwood, Dr Roma Cartwright and Mike Tymm for their invaluable help in researching and in understanding.

Clive Hebard for patiently answering all the inane questions.

Michael Fawcett for putting up with the tears and tantrums.

All the contributors to this book who gave their time so generously despite the huge emotional cost.

# CONTENTS

# INTRODUCTION

LOOK AROUND YOU. What can you see? Objects, people, distances – things that you can touch, or measure or verify in some other way. But what if someone were to tell you that there existed another dimension, outside of what you can see or hear or touch or quantify? A dimension that's all around us and within us, and yet largely invisible to us, where laws of space and time no longer operate. It is, this same helpful person might explain to you, the dimension that separates the consciousness from the physical. It is the dimension which your soul, your awareness, your ego, whatever it is you call the essence that is you, will inhabit when your flesh and blood body is dead or dying.

Of course, you'd want to have proof. You'd want to know how they could be so sure, so convinced. This is when the other person – perhaps someone you know well, someone you respect and trust – might look you steadily in the eyes and say, 'Because I've been there.'

LP Hartley famously wrote, 'The past is a foreign country, they do things differently there.' The same might well be said of death. It's a foreign country from which very few ever return. And, when they do, the rest of us are generally not interested in their slide shows or their snapshots or their souvenirs. Just as, though we might feign polite interest, we don't really want to hear at length about the trekking of the Himalayas or see endless home footage of our neighbour's Kenyan safari. By adulthood, our minds tend to be too flabby around the edges, too out of condition, too lazy even for anything that requires any great leap of imagination. We prefer the known, the irrefutable, the everyday.

Which is why these near-death survivors (although some would take issue with the 'near' part of that particular label) tend to keep quiet about their journeys, hugging their memories of that different world, that different dimension, close to their chests. But chances are you know someone who's been there. Maybe it's your neighbour, maybe someone at work, or your local policeman or your GP. There won't be any outward sign, no telltale suntan, no souvenir T-shirt, but this person will be going about his or her daily life – perhaps looking after their kids or drinking in the pub with friends, or just watching the TV – one hundred per cent certain they've had a foretaste of some kind of afterlife.

It could be somebody like Robert – a 44-year-old deputy head from Northamptonshire. See him teaching a Year Nine maths class or sitting in a staff meeting using his metal-framed glasses to emphasise a point, and you'd never imagine there was anything particularly unusual about him. But Robert has visited that other dimension, and it's something he'll never forget.

When Robert died in August 1995, his doctors were

horrified. But not half as horrified as Robert himself when he unexpectedly came back to life.

'I'd been in a place of such indescribable peace and calm that coming back into my body felt like the most terrible betrayal,' he admits. 'I died – if you want to be really dramatic you could say "flatlined" – on the operating table while I was having my appendix taken out. Apparently, I went into cardiac arrest as a reaction to the anaesthetic they used. It sounds bizarre now, although it didn't at the time, but I felt like I was floating a few feet above my body, looking down and seeing myself lying there surrounded by hospital staff. They were all panicking except this one nurse who hovered around nervously at the back as if she didn't quite know what she was supposed to be doing. She was very young and I remember feeling quite sorry for her. Then they were gone and I found myself facing this immense, intense light and a feeling of total and utter calm flooded through me. I don't have words to describe it, except to say that I felt completely and utterly safe, warm and happy. Imagine the most perfect, blissful feeling you've ever had and then multiply it by a thousand. Then, all of a sudden, there was a kind of whumping sound and I was back in my body with all these people fussing around and this crushing weight on my chest. It sounds ungrateful now, but at the time I felt totally cheated.'

But, if Robert thinks he had it bad, he should consider the famous case of poor George Rodonaia, a Soviet dissident knocked down in a suspicious car accident in 1976 whose own experience of otherworldly bliss was cut brutally short when someone started performing an autopsy on him!

'There I was, flooded with all these good things and this wonderful experience, when someone begins to cut into my stomach,' he told writer Phillip Berman in his book *The Journey Home*. 'Can you imagine? What had happened was that I was taken to the morgue. I was pronounced dead and left there for three days. An investigation into the cause of my death was set up, so they sent someone out to do an autopsy on me.'

Sounds like the plot of a farfetched sci-fi/horror movie. Yet Robert and George aren't mad or delusional. Nor, in Robert's case at least, would he describe himself as particularly spiritual. They're just people who have ventured into the jaws of death, into this other dimension... and back. And they're far from alone.

According to a 1997 US News and World Report, over 15 million people in America alone have, like Robert and George Rodonaia, had an NDE. That's one in twenty of the US population. And, because of the stigma often involved in admitting to such an experience, that figure is likely to be the tip of a very large iceberg. No such statistics exist for the UK, but researchers are convinced that, given the right encouragement to come forward, the numbers of people admitting to having left their bodies and undertaken spiritual journeys while hovering close to death would be staggering.

NDEs have been reported all over the world from wildly varying cultures. Though the language and imagery used is very different – as is the interpretation put upon the experience – there remain core similarities.

'I believe NDEs are more widespread than we know,' says nurse Penny Sartori, who has been researching NDE at Morriston Hospital Intensive Therapy Unit in South Wales.

'Out of the fifteen NDEs in my study, only two patients volunteered the information to me. The remaining thirteen would not have talked about the NDE had I not asked them. Many feared being disbelieved, ridiculed or they simply didn't understand the experience and put it down to a "trick of the mind".'

There are also numerous celebrities among those who have been brave enough to go public. Sharon Stone almost died from internal bleeding caused by a tear in an artery at the base of her skull and described seeing a giant vortex of white light and being met by friends before recovering. Peter Sellers admitted to an NDE during the first of eight heart attacks, reporting an incredibly beautiful, bright and loving light. Jane Seymour, too, saw a white light when she was undergoing an allergic reaction to an injection of penicillin.

So what defines an NDE? Basically, a near-death experience occurs when someone who appears clinically dead in terms of pulse, respiration, temperature, blood pressure and brain activity unexpectedly returns to life having had an 'otherworldly' experience. But, as some of the studies in this book reveal, it can also describe an experience where someone who should logically have died survives, in some cases with barely a scratch, again having passed through an 'otherworldly' phase. These experiences are all different, and yet typically they'll share one or more common NDE elements.

These elements might include floating above your physical body, going through a tunnel, experiencing a bright all-encompassing light which produces feelings of intense love and wellbeing, encountering deceased friends and relatives, seeing moments from your own life flash before you, then being informed it's not yet your time and sent back to your own body.

Some people experience several of these elements, others only one or two. More rarely the 'experiencer' will find no shared reference points at all. But, however tenuous the connections to other people's experiences, the knowledge that they are not alone in what they've been through comes as a tremendous relief to most NDE survivors, who often find themselves feeling isolated in their normal lives.

When Dr Raymond Moody, largely credited with being the Godfather of NDE, first began his pioneering research into the phenomenon in the 1970s, it was a relatively unknown subject. So imagine his astonishment when people he came across in his everyday life began admitting that, yes, they'd experienced the same thing.

'To my amazement, I found that, in almost every class of thirty or so students, at least one student would come to me afterwards and relate a personal near-death experience,' he writes in his groundbreaking 1975 work *Life After Life*.

Yet, while Moody may have been the one to give NDE its name, it was certainly not a new phenomenon when he came to write about it in the 1970s. Sure, advances in medical science and the growing trend of dying in hospital rather than at home meant that more critically ill patients were being successfully resuscitated – and therefore more likely to report an NDE. However, individual accounts of NDE have existed for centuries, even back to Plato whose 'Legend of Er' described the experience of a soldier who awoke on his own funeral pyre. What's striking about the pre-1970s NDE accounts isn't how different they are from the modern ones, including those in this book – but how similar. Take a look at this account which describes the experience of an anonymous physician as told to members of the Royal Medical Society during its bicentenary celebrations in 1937. The experience was related by Sir Auckland Geddes and reported in *The Scotsman* and the *Edinburgh Medical Journal*. It was also included in *The Last Crossing*, a book by one of the most celebrated psychics of the era, Gladys Osborne Leonard.

'On Saturday, 9 November, a few minutes after midnight, I began to feel very ill, and by two o'clock was definitely suffering from acute gastro-enteritis, which kept me vomiting and purging until about eight o'clock.

'By ten o'clock I had developed all the symptoms of very acute poisoning; intense gastro-intestinal pain, diarrhoea; pulse and respirations becoming quite impossible to count. I wanted to ring for assistance, but found I could not, and so quite placidly gave up the attempt. I realised I was very ill and very quickly reviewed my whole financial position; thereafter at no time did my consciousness appear to me to be in any way dimmed, but I suddenly realised that my consciousness was separating from another consciousness, which was also me…

'Gradually I realised that I could see not only my body and the bed in which it was, but everything in the whole house and garden, and I then realised that I was seeing not only "things" at home, but in London and in Scotland, in fact wherever my attention was directed it seemed to me…

'I saw "A" enter my bedroom. I realised she got a terrible shock and I saw her hurry to the telephone. I saw my doctor leave his patients and come very quickly, and heard him say, or saw him think, "He's nearly gone." I heard him quite clearly speaking to me on the bed, but I was not in touch with the body, and could not answer him. I was really cross when he took a syringe and rapidly injected my body with something which I afterwards learned was camphor. As the heart began to beat more strongly, I was drawn back and I was intensely annoyed because I was so interested, and just beginning to understand where I was and what I was "seeing". I came back into the body really angry at being pulled back, and once I was back all the clarity of vision of anything and everything disappeared, and I was just possessed of a glimmer of consciousness which was suffused with pain.

'It is surprising to note that this dream, vision or experience has shown no tendency to fade like a dream would fade. Nor has it shown any tendency that I am aware of to grow or to rationalise itself as a dream would do. I think that the whole thing simply means that, but for medical treatment of a peculiarly prompt and vigorous kind, I was dead to the three-dimensional universe. If this is so, and if, in fact, the experience of liberation of consciousness in the fourth dimensional universe is not imagination, it is a most important matter to place on record.'

It's all very familiar – the dividing of the conscious from the physical, the freedom of being in that other dimension, unconstrained by space and time, the sense of disappointment at being brought 'back'. And yet this was seventy years ago – nearly forty years before Moody coined the phrase NDE. The author of the 1937 account preferred to remain anonymous, no doubt worried about the effect going public would have on his professional standing. The tragedy is that, seven decades on, little has changed.

There continues to be a blanket of secrecy around the whole near-death experience phenomenon – a blanket which stifles and smothers the feelings and concerns of those who go through this most life-changing of events, and are left searching for answers and for credibility.

So why the deafening silence? Well, one word sums it up. One little word that packs a huge scary punch. Death.

Though we don't like to admit it, death is still the ultimate taboo. We tiptoe around terminally ill patients using well-meaning phrases like 'you're a fighter' and 'if anyone can beat this, you can', thereby turning death into an adversary and people who die into losers. Death is seen as the end. The big sleep. The void. All alternative visions are dismissed as the realm of religious fanatics and new-agers who overshot the drugs runway.

We spend billions of pounds keeping dying patients alive for a few extra days or weeks, prolonging their agony in exchange for a few more precious moments of life. According to some estimates an incredible eighty per cent of England's clinical NHS budget is spent on patients who'll die within three months. And we do that because life is everything and death is seen as the ultimate full stop.

When Penny Sartori first started working in the Intensive Therapy Unit in 1993, she was shocked at the doctors' attitude to death.

'Some patients were obviously dying but the doctors would do everything they could to keep that patient alive.'

So, given the prevailing refusal to think of death as anything but a defeat, it's not surprising that NDEs – with their premise that death is the beginning of the journey rather than the end – aren't exactly what the doctor ordered.

Yet some scientists are daring to say the unthinkable – that near-death experiences, far from belonging on the lunatic fringes along with crop circles and alien abductions, merit more research and more serious debate.

In 2001 *The Lancet* published the results of a ten-year survey by a team of doctors in the Netherlands who had interviewed 344 patients who were resuscitated after cardiac arrest left them technically 'dead'. Of these, sixty-two told of a near-death experience, with forty-one describing it as 'deep'. The fact that there were no medical or physiological factors unifying those who had NDEs and those who didn't mystified the doctors. The experiences couldn't be blamed on delusions brought about by a certain medication, or physical cause. And the fact that patients who had been clinically dead brought back such clear memories, even of what had been going on in the resuscitation room around their lifeless bodies, left the doctors facing a hitherto unimaginable hypothesis – that consciousness might not be located in the brain.

From there it's just a short step to the question: if our consciousness and awareness of who and where we are isn't located in the brain, might there be a chance that it also doesn't 'die' with the brain?

This is the crux of the near-death experience debate. Are people who 'come back from the dead' talking about tunnels, beings of light and meetings with deceased relatives simply recounting fantasies brought on in the seconds before 'dying' by medications or brain chemicals or the body's natural reaction to trauma? Or have they really been offered a glimpse into another realm of consciousness to which death isn't the barrier but the gateway?

If it's the latter, it has huge repercussions on how we treat our dying, Penny Sartori believes. 'When I came across NDEs, I thought, "If this is really what death is like why do we spend so much time, effort and resources on patients who are clearly dying?"' she says. 'It was a particular encounter with a dying patient that made me think, "Is death really that bad that we must do all we can to keep patients alive even if they want to die?"'

The late Elisabeth Kubler-Ross, the highly respected psychiatrist and author of *On Life After Death*, spoke to many dying patients and heard deathbed accounts which convinced her that there might indeed be life after physical death.

'It is evident from [Raymond Moody's] findings that the dying patient continues to have a conscious awareness of his environment after being pronounced clinically dead,' she writes in her foreword to Moody's *Life After Life*. 'This very much coincides with my own research, which has used the accounts of patients who have died and made a comeback, totally against our expectations and often to the surprise of some highly sophisticated, well-known and certainly accomplished physicians.'

Kubler-Ross became a world-renowned champion of the right to die with dignity and brought the hospice movement into the mainstream, arguing that death shouldn't be battled with, but rather accepted and even enjoyed as a transition into another state of being.

But, for every scientist trying to shed light into the darkness of death, there are thousands more who refuse to see NDE as anything more than a by-product of a traumatised and confused physical body.

When NDEs were first brought to public attention, the accepted scientific wisdom was that they were the delusions of people on the brink of death who saw 'on the other side' what they wanted to see.

It's easy to see why such a view was fashionable. Inevitably people who've been through NDE tend to put their own spin on it. So the bright light that produces unconditional love often becomes Christ or Buddha or God, or whichever explanation fits that person's cultural background.

And yet, the flaws in that argument are obvious. Not all experiencers had any kind of religious background (although atheists have sometimes found themselves holding strong spiritual/religious beliefs and convictions after the event). And, if these people are just seeing what they're expecting from death, why don't they all see the same thing?

Jackie, a 57-year-old grandmother from Essex who 'died' after a pulmonary embolism, told me of her surprise in being greeted 'on the other side' not by a close relative as she'd always imagined, but someone she'd not seen for decades.

'It was the old man, our neighbour, who used to bring his dog to meet me from the bus stop after school when I was little,' she says. 'He'd hold out his hand to me to help me down and walk me back to my house, but he died when I was about twelve. When I was lying in the hospital with no apparent heartbeat, he was the one I saw, reaching his hand out, just as he used to. Only when I tried to take his hand I couldn't reach it. I kept trying, but I couldn't. Then he shook his head and suddenly I was back in my body. It's so strange because I honestly hadn't thought of him in years.'

Negative NDEs also cast doubt on the theory that life-threatening events cause us to see our own version of 'heaven'. Andy, a restaurant manager from Canada who was protective of his identity to the point of paranoia, sent me this account of his terrifying NDE.

'This was in 1988; I was twenty-seven and just married. I was in my parents' house, running down a flight of stairs with my dog who was chasing a tennis ball. I slipped on the ball and descended the rest of the flight on my back (about ten steps). I had the wind knocked out of me and could breathe out but not in. I was in tremendous pain. I knew I was dying, but surprisingly, I was totally calm inside, knowing there was absolutely nothing I could do about it. This surprised me, because I had always thought that I would be very upset when my time came to die. I gasped out to my wife to call an ambulance and collapsed on to the floor.

'The next thing I experienced was like getting up, out of bed; I simply rose up from my supine position, and could see the room I was in, but it was like looking at everything through a purple haze. I was totally pain-free, but fully conscious, and I thought to myself, "I must have dreamed that I fell down the stairs and hurt my back, because I feel fine." I looked at the washing machine and dryer and moved around a little with the sensation of floating, but then I felt myself moving quickly in one direction out of the room, along what seemed to be a type of corridor, still through a purple haze. Suddenly I saw hundreds of people's faces appearing along the corridor sides. They looked very angry at me and were pointing their fingers accusingly at me, shouting, "Get back! What are you doing here? It's not your time yet!"

'I was absolutely terrified at their response to my presence and backed away quickly, which gave me a sense of falling downwards. I then heard a loud "POP" and felt a rush of pain flooding into my consciousness. I jumped up and saw that I was back where I had fallen. My wife, who was standing near by and saw the whole thing which lasted about a minute, said that I had the most terrified look in my eyes and was screaming, "NO! GET AWAY FROM ME! LEAVE ME ALONE!" as I jumped up. She thought I was shouting at her and backed away.

'I ran out of the house to wait for the ambulance and stood barefeet in jeans and a T-shirt, in Canadian mid-January weather, but feeling totally comfortable until the ambulance arrived. I was X-rayed at the hospital and found to have badly bruised vertebrae but, thank God, nothing broken. I took about three months to totally recover from the pain, but I never really gave my experience a second thought until about three years later when I stumbled across books on NDE at the bookstore and read about other people's experiences.'

Andy was a young man playing with his dog. He wasn't having some kind of spiritual crisis and certainly hadn't gone looking for the kind of nightmarish otherworldly scenario he describes. Nor did he invest his experience with any kind of significance afterwards. In other words, he was neither attention seeking nor looking for some kind of validation of already held beliefs.

So cultural conditioning can't explain away NDE nor give any insight into why so many people who are supposedly clinically dead are able to describe with such accuracy what was going on around their lifeless bodies.

Neither can it explain the transformative effects NDEs often have on the lives of people who live through them. One-time entrepreneur Dannion Brinkley devoted his life to helping the dying after being struck by lightning while on the telephone and ending up in the morgue. Donna Desoto, who 'died' following a stroke and made a promise during her subsequent NDE to help children, went on to set up SavBaby, a charity which rescues abandoned infants.

But for each of these well-known cases there are many more who come back from the dead altered in subtler, but no less meaningful ways. Ken Mullens, René Turner and Harry Hone, all of whom tell their stories in this book, returned with a real evangelical zeal to help others lose their fear of death. Others, like American Dan Williams, undergo a private religious conversion as a result of what they have seen, as he explains: 'I grew up in a wealthy family. My father was a respected attorney, politician and author, my grandfather was a famous major general in the Army. I was destined to be something special. By my mid-twenties, I was already a college director. Then an addiction to prescription and street drugs lost me everything. I was penniless and was stealing drugs to support my habit. I went to drug-treatment centres at least nine times but never could get clean. I was charged with over twelve felony drug charges, as well as several DUI charges. I had given up on attempts to get clean and sober; I had pretty much given up on life. I was arrested over two years ago again and was told by substance-abuse doctors and counsellors that, after fifteen years of daily pill abuse, sudden withdrawal from drugs while in prison would mean I would probably die from the rebound effect [withdrawals]. I prepared to die in jail. On the seventh day in jail, during a seizure, my heart stopped; they found me in my cell, revived me and sent me to the hospital. But, while my heart had stopped, my soul, spirit or consciousness did not die. It was amazing! I dealt with many issues during a review of my life and also dealt with my addiction, among other things. It is hard to describe what actually happened but I have not desired a drug since. My life has purpose since this spiritual experience. I am a completely different person.'

It's hard to believe that something that was a culturally dictated delusion could bring about such complete and lasting transformation. Other scientific theories are similarly unable to account for all the different and mystifying elements of NDE. The sceptic's favourite is the one about NDE being the creation of disturbed brain chemistry brought about by certain medications, lack of oxygen or changes in carbon dioxide.

However, in the scientific studies that have been done, there's no evidence that the patients who have powerful near-death experiences have any lower oxygen levels or different combinations of drugs than those who experienced nothing.

Dr Sam Parnia, Fellow in Pulmonary and Critical Care Medicine at Cornell University, New York, and Honorary Research Fellow at Southampton University, is one of the new breed of scientists pushing for more research to be done into the whole NDE phenomenon.

'There has been this perception in the public mind that, although NDEs are interesting, the causes are all done and dusted – it's all down to lack of oxygen. End of story. And yet that completely discounts the different studies that have been done which show consciousness continues even when there's severe interruption to blood flow and brain flow.'

Dr Parnia is trying to raise funds for a comprehensive study of cardiac arrest subjects using a machine that measures brain activity. If patients revive following a cardiac arrest and are able to describe events happening around them at the exact time that no brain activity was being recorded by the machine, it has far-reaching implications for scientific debate into the whole phenomenon of NDE.

'It's a way of testing the potential that there could be a separation of consciousness from the brain which happens at the end of life,' says Dr Parnia.

Another very popular theory from the sceptics is the so-called Ketamine Connection. Ketamine is a powerful drug sometimes used as an anaesthetic during invasive surgery because it enables the patient to distance himself from his own body by partially blocking N-P receptors which are involved in thinking, memory, emotion, language, sensation and perception. It also produces delusions or hallucinations which include many of the elements reported in NDEs. Patients given ketamine have reported tunnels, bright lights and out-of-body experiences. From this, some scientists, most notably Dr Karl Jansen, have hypothesised that perhaps the brain releases a ketamine-like chemical when subjected to extreme trauma or stress.

However, further research has shown significant differences between NDE and ketamine-induced experience. Ornella Corazza, a research scholar at the University of Tokyo as well as at SOAS in London, has studied forty cases of people who've tried dissociative anaesthia such as ketamine and compared their accounts to those of NDE subjects who'd been interviewed by NDE expert Dr Peter Fenwick after suffering cardiac arrest.

'Although the "core" features of the experience were the same (tunnel, light, strong feeling of dying, meeting with "Beings of

Light"), a few significant differences emerged,' she reports. 'For instance, the ketamine (or simply "K") group was less inclined to see the light (only 20% reached this final stage – it was 70% in Fenwick's study), to meet "others" (16% against 57% in Fenwick's study), to reach a point of no return (46% versus 70%). On the contrary, the K-group experienced a much stronger sense of cosmic union (50% against 20% in Fenwick's study).'

Many of those who have looked into the question of drug-induced NDEs versus natural ones also point out that the two are not mutually exclusive – that the existence of one doesn't disprove the existence of the other. Drug-induced NDEs merely underline the argument that there exists a separation of the consciousness from the physical – but one doesn't necessarily have to 'die' to experience it.

So, despite theories, we don't seem to be much nearer to uncovering the definitive truth behind the proliferation of NDE accounts. The one great advance is that, after decades on the margins of the scientific radar (if not out of range entirely), scientists now seem to be more willing to engage with the mere notion that there's something out there worth studying.

Dr Jeffrey Long, a physician specialising in radiation oncology (the use of radiation to treat cancer) in Tacoma, Washington, has seen many changes since he helped found the NDE Research Foundation (NDERF) which now has the largest selection of published accounts of near-death experiences in the world. 'Several years ago, I performed an e-mail survey of the entire medical staff of a major academic medical school regarding physician attitudes about NDE,' he says.

'The survey confirmed my impression that there is still a great deal of misunderstanding and scepticism about NDE. The main problem, in my opinion, is that NDE is so different from our normal everyday experiences that it is difficult for scientists and physicians to accept that these experiences actually do happen. Our website archives contain a large number of accounts from scientists and physicians who had an NDE. Those scientists and physicians experiencing NDE certainly generally believe their experience was real. I think there is increasing acceptance of NDE in the scientific and medical community over the years. There are dozens of credible publications in the scientific literature regarding NDE, and I think this wave of publications is very slowly starting to change attitudes.'

Dr Sam Parnia has also noticed this change. 'In the 1970s, consciousness was considered as falling solely into the area of theology. Now, finally, scientists are seeing it as worthy of scientific exploration.'

As society shifts from shutting out everything for which there are no answers to recognising that there's value merely in exploring the questions themselves, so NDE is finally coming in from the cold.

In fact, so mainstream is it becoming that there's even a generic NDE joke involving a middle-aged woman who has a near-death experience in hospital after suffering a heart attack. During that experience she sees God who tells her – in typical NDE fashion – that it isn't yet her time and that, actually, she has another thirty or forty years to live.

Thus assured of living into a ripe old age, the woman then decides to make the most of it. She stays on in hospital after recovering from the heart attack and undergoes major cosmetic surgery – face-lift, liposuction, boob job and a tummy tuck. She even has someone come in and change her hair colour. She reckons she's got the time, so she might as well make the most of it.

Stepping out of the hospital feeling like a million dollars, she is immediately killed by a speeding ambulance. Arriving once again in front of God, she is seething. 'I thought you said I had another thirty or forty years,' she demands.

'Sorry,' God replies. 'I didn't recognise you.'

Twenty years ago, nobody took NDE seriously. Now we're starting to take it so seriously we're even able to joke about it! Slowly, public figures are starting to come forward to tell their own stories of NDE. Entertainers such as Jane Seymour, Elizabeth Taylor and Ozzy Osbourne have all described their own experience of life at the point of death. And recently former president Bill Clinton described how, during heart surgery, he saw 'circles of light' containing the faces of his wife and daughter, flying towards a 'brightness'. 'I'm not quite sure whether it was one of those "near-death experiences",' he wrote in *Parade Magazine* in 2005, 'or a life-affirming one – perhaps it was a bit of both.'

As NDE shifts into the mainstream, the hope is that it will shed much of the stigma that currently clings to it. While most of the subjects in this book have agreed to use their full names, hoping that by speaking out they can help promote healthy debate and discussion about the whole NDE question, and maybe end up with some answers of their own, others have insisted on changing their identities.

'Gabi', a self-employed business coach, worries that her clients might think her less professional if they found out about her operating table drama. 'Sam' has never found the right time to talk to his parents about the truth behind his suicide attempt, his NDE and how his life has unfolded since. 'Georgina', whose brother spent time in prison following his brutal attack on her, worries about jeopardising already fragile family truces. Everyone has their reasons. Everyone has their secrets.

So NDE isn't quite out of the closet yet. Though we've made progress in our willingness to listen and understand since Dr Raymond Moody first started writing, these have been small pigeon steps rather than great strides. And, for every person willing to tell their story, there are still thousands or hundreds of thousands, who keep quiet for fear of ridicule – or worse.

That's why the accounts in this book are all in the first person. To give voice to those who might otherwise not be heard. To allow people to talk openly, many for the first time, about what remains, for most of them, the defining experience of their lives.

# 1

## PAUL TUCKER, 27
### FINANCIAL ADVISER, NORTH LONDON

IF ANY OF my mates knew I'd had a near-death experience, I'd never hear the end of it. I'm not joking. I work in a large financial institution in London. It's practically an all-male environment and, believe me, it's not the kind of thing you throw into conversation. 'By the way, I died and left my body and floated around the universe a bit. Oh, and make mine a double.'

You can just imagine the reaction, can't you? I mean, most of the people I know would feel more comfortable if you'd told them you had bird flu than if you said you'd had any kind of spiritual experience. It's just the environment I'm in.

And, let's be honest, I'd have been exactly the same before this happened. Up until October 2004, I was as cynical as they come. I remember having an argument in the office, just days before my accident, with one of the secretaries who'd spent a fortune going to see a clairvoyant during the lunch hour. She wanted to find out if this bloke she'd just started seeing was 'The One'.

When she got back, we all started taking the piss out of her, but especially me.

'Well, how do you explain the fact that she knew about my uncle dying of lung cancer?' she'd asked me, really rattled. 'And she gave me a message from him to tell my auntie not to worry.'

Of course, I'd been really dismissive, telling her it was just a lucky guess.

'Where's the proof?' I asked her. 'There isn't any. I'm sorry but, when you're dead, you're dead.'

To be honest with you, I'm still not sure what I think about clairvoyants and things like that. I think there are a lot of people out there making money out of vulnerable people. But one thing I do know for sure now – when you're dead, you're not always dead.

If that sounds crazy, I'm really sorry. There just isn't any way of putting it that doesn't sound like I should be locked up in the nearest psychiatric facility. That's why I don't tell anybody. Well, at least nobody from work.

It was 16 October 2004 and I was spending the weekend with a friend, Jason, and his girlfriend Karen, who have a weekend cottage in Sussex. We'd arrived the night before and we'd spent the evening getting plastered in the local pub, so the next morning I decided I needed to do something wholesome and outdoorsy to make up for it. Don't you just hate that feeling you get after you've really overdone things, like you're just this great big horrible blob? I can't stand it.

At first Jason wasn't too keen on the idea of getting up at the crack of dawn (well, okay, ten in the morning) but in the end I

24

managed to drag him out of bed, and he grudgingly agreed to join me on a bike ride. The weather was pretty grim, but I just really wanted to be out and about. I was riding Karen's bike, so of course there was a lot of piss-taking about how poncy I looked (even though the bike was black it had this pink writing on it).

We'd ridden for about a mile or so when we came to this big hill. Getting up it was a real slog, particularly with a massive hangover. Jason was suffering more than I was so he fell further and further behind. I was really panting by the time I got to the top and was wishing I'd remembered to bring some water with me.

I remember stopping for a moment on top of the hill. Looking back, I could see Jason had got off his bike and was pushing it uphill.

'Lightweight!' I shouted at him, but I don't know whether he heard.

Ahead of me, the road sloped downhill, lined with hedges on either side and it looked even steeper than the hill we'd just come up. I remember feeling one of those rushes of anticipation, just like being a kid again, at the thought of flying down that hill on the bike. Jason had said there was another village about a mile and a half further on, and I was already looking forward to a lunchtime pint. So much for being virtuous!

I pushed off down the hill, letting the bike pick up speed as I went on. It had been raining earlier and the road was slightly wet, so I knew I should be cautious. But it was so exhilarating I just couldn't bring myself to slow it down. Anyway, it was a country road and there were no cars around.

At the bottom of the hill there was a junction. Don't ask me why but I assumed I'd have the right of way there. By the time

I got close enough to see the give-way sign, which had helpfully been twisted round slightly so you didn't see it straight off, it was too late to stop, especially with the ground being so wet. To be honest, I didn't really think there was much of a risk anyway. We'd only passed three or four cars the whole time we'd been cycling and it wasn't exactly a major junction. 'I'd have to be pretty unlucky for something to be coming just the second I go across,' I thought.

Well, guess what? I was just that unlucky.

Because of the high hedges, I couldn't see the traffic on the road that crossed over until I was practically at the junction. There was a split second as I flew past the end of the hedge on my right and noticed a big dark-coloured estate car approaching, very fast.

'Oh shit,' I said. Or maybe I just thought it.

There was a cracking sound on impact, and I hit the windscreen of the car and was thrown about twenty feet through the air. I don't really remember feeling anything during the time I was in motion, it all happened so fast.

Then I felt this kind of 'pop'. I really don't know how to describe it any better than that. When I talked to my sister (who's the only person I've ever told) about it, she said it sounded like when she was in labour and her waters broke, but I'll just have to take her word for that!

Anyway, after this 'pop' I suddenly found myself about six feet off the ground, looking down on someone lying on his back. I remember thinking, 'I don't rate his chances much', because this bloke was lying in a really awkward position with his right leg sticking out at the knee in a really unnatural way and blood coming from his ears and head.

It was a while before I realised that the guy was wearing the same jeans as me, same jacket and, oh blimey, it *was* me. But, even once I'd realised that, I wasn't really upset, just fascinated watching myself lying there and wondering what would happen next.

I didn't even feel particularly shocked to be hovering in the air. I remember being aware of the fact that the 'me' that was up above the ground didn't appear to have any legs or arms or physical shape at all, but it didn't seem to bother me. In fact, I rather liked it. It felt liberating. I felt really relaxed and comfortable, and not at all stressed out like you'd imagine. It was sort of like you'd feel if you were lying back at home on your sofa surrounded by cushions, with something you really wanted to watch on the TV.

The woman who'd been driving the estate ran out of her car and knelt down next to me. She was saying, 'Oh my God, oh my God' over and over again. I looked at her car. The windscreen had shattered, but it had held together and there was a big dent where my body had hit it. In the backseat there was a small child crying and shouting 'Mummy, Mummy'. I think he or she must have been strapped into a car seat because they didn't get out, just sat there crying. The driver's door was wide open where the woman had got out in a hurry and the car stereo was still on, blasting out that Katie Melua song 'Closest Thing to Crazy'. Before the accident I quite liked that song. Now I can't listen to it at all and have to leave the room if anyone puts it on.

I had no sense of time when I was hovering about, but at some point Jason arrived and joined the woman kneeling next to me – or rather to my body on the ground.

'What happened?' he yelled at her. 'What have you done?'

He was crying and shaking, and she looked really scared. I felt really bad then because it hadn't been the woman's fault. I wanted to tell her it was okay. I wanted to tell them both that I was fine and they shouldn't be crying over me. But I couldn't speak, or else they couldn't hear me.

Another car drove up then, with a middle-aged couple inside. The woman stayed in the car while the man got out and ran over to where I was lying.

'Is he dead?' he asked.

To my surprise, Jason nodded. I remember feeling really shocked. How could I be dead, when I felt so good? And, if I really was dead, where was I now?

Then all of a sudden I wasn't at the road any more. I was in this big kind of funnel that was rotating. It was sort of like you'd imagine being inside one of those giant car-wash things that spiral round and round. It was dark, but there was a light coming through from the top, as if it was daylight – but really bright sunlight, not the grey day it had just been.

Again I wasn't scared at this. I just wanted to get out because I really wanted to be in that sunlight and out of this funnel thing. I moved to the top, but I don't really know how. I didn't have arms or legs, but I just kind of thought myself into motion. It's really hard to explain.

Then I was out into the sunlight. It felt unbelievable, just indescribable. I just felt completely happy, one hundred per cent content. Have you ever gone on holiday when it's winter back home and freezing cold and wet and it starts getting dark at 3pm? If you imagine how it feels to get off the plane the other end and walk out into that blast of hot sunshine after all those months of being cold and miserable, and then imagine something a million times better, you might get close to how I felt when I went into that light.

It felt like everything had clicked into place. I hadn't really ever been aware of feeling like I didn't quite belong, or wasn't quite in the right place, and yet when I was in the light I realised what it was like to feel completely a part of everything around you, completely comfortable in what you are and where you are. It was like that feeling you get when you know you've given someone the best present in the world – that warm feeling of having got something completely right.

I couldn't really see anything in the light, it was too bright. But I became aware of presences around me – fuzzy shapes moving around on the edge of my vision. But they weren't frightening at all. I felt really reassured by them. I knew they were totally on my side.

One of these shapes spoke to me, only it wasn't words, more like thoughts that were immediately transferred into my head.

'Are you ready?' it asked.

I felt really pleased then, really happy. But, before I could answer, I found myself in a different scene altogether. I was in a dark room, somewhere up near the ceiling and I was looking down on a lot of people all in dark clothes. There was a strange noise coming from somewhere, like an animal in distress, but I couldn't see where it was coming from.

I recognised my mum and dad at the front of the room. My mum was wearing a dress I'd never seen before and she looked like she'd lost about a stone in weight. Her whole face looked sunken inwards, like someone had put a drawstring around the edges and pulled it tightly in towards the middle. Her eyes were red and she just stared out towards the front. I remember noticing that she had a line of grey in her hair at the parting and I was really surprised because my mother always gets her hair done religiously every four weeks – she says she'd rather leave the house naked than with any grey hair showing.

My dad was next to her with his head bowed. From where I was above and slightly to the front of them, I could see his shoulders moving up and down and I realised he was crying. Then I also realised that the strange noise was coming from him! He was sobbing these huge grating, gasping sobs. I could feel the embarrassment and awkwardness of the people in the row behind him and I felt full of sadness suddenly. I'd never seen my dad cry before.

My sister was sitting on the other side of my mum, holding her hand tightly with tears streaming down her face. And next to her was a young woman I didn't know. She too had her head bent so I couldn't see her face, just the top of her long brown hair which was tied back in a ponytail. I remember the elastic band it was tied back with was bright pink which really stood out because everyone was wearing such dark clothes. I wondered who she was, but at the same time she seemed familiar and I felt like I should know her. It was very strange. Her shoulders were also shaking and she was obviously crying.

My heart felt really heavy as I was watching this scene. I felt overwhelmed with pity for my family and with guilt for having caused all their sadness.

I turned away and found myself back in the light once more.

'I have to go back,' I said to the shapes in the brightness – and immediately there was a loud whooshing sound and I was back inside my body. Only I wasn't by the side of the road any more; I was in a hospital bed and my dad was sitting on a chair next to me.

'What are you doing here?' I asked him.

Well, the poor guy almost had a heart attack on the spot! Here he was sitting with his practically dead son who'd been scraped off the road in pieces and had lain in a coma for three days. And whose chances of survival had been put about as high as Tim Henman's chances of winning Wimbledon (just watch, he'll go and do it now) and suddenly I'm asking what he's doing there.

His face cracked into a smile so big you'd think he had a coat hanger in his mouth, and then he bolted out of the door to call the doctors.

By the time they arrived, I was sincerely regretting my decision to come back. My body felt like it had been pulverised with a giant meat hammer. My right leg, which had broken in three places, was in plaster, so it didn't hurt, but the rest of me was in agony.

Apparently, I'd punctured my left lung, fractured my skull and ribs and burst both ear drums. I'd also sustained severe lacerations to the head and body. In addition there was unknown damage to my brain, although thankfully that has turned out to be minimal. Paramedics from the ambulance that brought me to hospital had thought I was dead when they first arrived on the scene, but had then discovered a very faint pulse. Even so, they'd thought they'd 'lost' me a couple of times on the way to the hospital, and when I arrived there I was pretty close to dead. Apparently, when Jason had rung my mum and dad to tell them about the accident, he hadn't been able to speak and my dad had had to prompt him, saying, 'Is it bad news?' to which Jason, ever the optimist, had replied, 'The worst.' Which just shows you how much faith he had in me. Even the doctors hadn't rated my chances very high, giving my parents that old 'where there's life, there's hope' line. So, when I woke up from my three-day coma, I was, well, pretty much a mess.

After the blissful freedom I'd felt during my near-death experience, to find myself back in this brutally battered body felt really cruel. At any time over the next few weeks while I slowly recovered, I think I'd have gone back on my decision given half a chance. But slowly I did start to feel better. Every day brought new advances. Hey, I can roll over without feeling like I've stabbed myself in the chest. Hey, I can actually hear what people are saying. Woo-hoo.

I was discharged from hospital five and a half weeks after my accident. Even though I'd been living on my own for six years, I went back to my parents' house in Surrey to recuperate. I was a bit like a baby at that time, not just physically, but also emotionally. I felt really shaky and needed constant reassurance.

Gradually, with time (and plenty of my mum's home cooking), I got stronger and started to go out again near my mum and dad's house. I was still not walking properly but I felt much better. It was on my first night out that I met Melissa who has just become my fiancée.

I don't know about love at first sight, but there was something about her that just drew me to her and we felt comfortable with one another right from the word go. Even after one date, I knew she was the girl I wanted to marry. And yes, she does have brown hair. Weirdly, even though it was short when we met, I later found out she'd only had it cut a few weeks before. At the time of my accident it would have been long, just like the girl I'd seen in the church.

But I don't want to read too much into that, and I haven't yet talked to her about it. Don't want to scare the poor girl off – at least not before the wedding! And anyway, there are a lot of girls with long brown hair in England. In fact, the only person I've ever told about all this is my sister. I didn't mean to tell her – it just came pouring out one evening when we were at a pub near my parents' house. She was cool about it though. I expect that's why I told her – because she's always been pretty open-minded and I knew she wouldn't think I was barmy.

I'm now back in my own flat in London and I'm almost back to normal. Apart from the fact that my short-term memory is pretty abysmal, I escaped without any lasting brain damage, which is pretty much a miracle, considering I wasn't wearing a helmet at the time. And my leg has never really healed properly. In fact, doctors are talking about re-breaking it in order to set it again, so you can imagine how happy that makes me. Not!

The NDE hasn't had much impact on the way I live. I know I'm supposed to say I gave up working in finance and gave over my life to helping starving children in Africa, but that wouldn't exactly be true. I love my job and I love the lifestyle that it gives me. As long as I still enjoy work, I'll carry on doing it. But I'm much more balanced than I was before my accident. I don't put in the mad hours I used to do. I've got my priorities much more sorted now and I spend a lot more time at home with Melissa and my family.

And I've turned into one of those annoying 'love ya' people. You know what I mean, I can't end a phone conversation or go out of the door without telling people that I love them. You never know when you're going to pop your clogs so I treat every goodbye as if it could be the last. I don't mean I have a huge farewell scene like Leonardo DiCaprio in *Titanic*, just that, when I do go, I don't want to leave anything unsaid.

But I don't worry about death. Not any more. I have no regrets about choosing to live because I'm really enjoying my life at the moment and I think I've got a lot of good things in store. I can't wait to get married and have kids.

But, when I have to die, I'm ready for it. In fact, I'm looking forward to it. Just not yet. Okay?

# 2

## GABI HALL, 37
### BUSINESS COACH, HERTFORDSHIRE

THE DAY BEFORE I went into hospital, I had a horrible premonition. It was an image, a kind of flash that came into my head without any warning, and, once it was there, I couldn't get rid of it.

In a panic, I called up my twin sister. 'I'm going to die on the operating table tomorrow,' I told her dramatically. 'I just know it.'

Danielle wasn't impressed. 'Don't be ridiculous, you're only getting your wisdom teeth out,' she said exasperated.

I knew it sounded stupid, but I just couldn't shake it, this feeling that something was going to go horribly wrong. It was as if everything in my life had been leading up towards this moment. It was part of some larger plan, and there was nothing I could do about it.

I've always been a little bit 'psychic'. Growing up, I'd often sensed something was going to happen before it did. And also, being a twin, I'd had a connection with my sister that meant I knew what she was thinking, and could tell she was going to call before the phone even rang.

But this premonition was different. Really scary. I managed to persuade Danielle to take the day off work and come to the hospital with me. But, after putting the phone down to her, I still didn't feel completely reassured.

'Just get a grip, Gabi,' I told myself sternly, but it was no use. That night, I lay awake for hours in my north London home, worrying about what the following day would bring. I tried to take my mind off it, reminding myself just how many people went through minor operations like this every day, but even so the nagging fear never left and I tossed and turned until the sky started to get light.

The next day, 17 June 1996, I arrived at the well-known London hospital where I was due to have my operation, still with a feeling of great trepidation. Danielle kept trying to make jokes to take my mind off it, but, even while I was laughing, my insides were still tensed up, like someone was squeezing them.

As soon as I walked into the operating theatre and was introduced to the team, I told them all about the premonition. I didn't care if they thought I was completely mad, I wanted them all – the surgeon, the anaesthetist, everybody – to know in advance that something was going to go wrong. At least that way they'd be prepared.

Of course, they just tried to pacify me, telling me this was just a routine operation, nothing to be afraid of.

'You'll be fine, Gabi,' Danielle told me, giving my arm a squeeze as she went out to wait in the waiting room. With a sickening feeling in my stomach, I wondered if that might be the last time I would see her.

As I was lying on the operating table, the surgeon explained what would happen and then the anaesthetist asked me to start counting backwards from ten. I think I got to about six before everything went black.

Then suddenly I was leaving my body and floating up to the ceiling. I didn't really feel scared, just sort of interested. I couldn't see my own physical body, it was more like I sensed I was out of it. I was still me, but you just couldn't see me. Does that make sense?

Then I went into a dark space where there were grey figures sitting in front of me. I didn't exactly 'see' them, more like I sensed they were there. And, when they spoke, I didn't 'hear' them, it was more like we were talking telepathically. It was like they were on a panel, and I felt they were judging me. I can only describe it as being like a weird spiritual job interview. People have asked me whether this was 'God'. But it wasn't one all-consuming being – rather a presence of beings if that makes any sense.

I wasn't frightened, but nor did I feel flooded with unconditional love and light like some other experiences I've read about. It was more like I'd gone through into another room and was chatting to these people.

'You have to go back,' they said to me. 'You have a mission.'

I remember not wanting to go back. I was going through a horrible time in my life, with lots of things going wrong, and I felt like it would all be so much easier if I could just stay where I was.

But then I was back in my body, and when I opened my eyes

the entire surgical team was in tears. Apparently, my premonition had come true – I'd died right there on the operating table.

'I told you that would happen,' I said, accusingly, sitting up.

They were all stunned to hear me speak.

'But we've given you more adrenaline than would kill a six-foot man,' the anaesthetist told me, incredulous.

They told me I'd had a massive anaphylactic shock in reaction to the muscle relaxant they'd given me. Whereas with normal anaphylactic shock you'd suffer a fit, I went straight into flatline. They were convinced they'd lost me and, in desperation, gave me a huge dose of adrenaline.

No one could believe it when I sat up, very much alive.

I could see my sister by the bed, also in tears. When the nurse had gone to break the news to her, the first thing she'd said was: 'She's had a heart attack, hasn't she?' Despite her earlier confidence, she'd had a strong feeling that the operation wasn't going as planned.

She later described going through to the operating room to see me as like 'watching your own death'. By that stage my body had gone into trauma as a result of the amount of histamine in it and had swelled up like a balloon. As we look so alike, it had seemed to Danielle as though she was watching herself on that table, struggling for life.

Incredibly, I pulled through and was released from hospital the following day. That should have been the happy ending, but it wasn't.

In the days and weeks after my operation, I went into a total decline. I felt like I was in a very dark place where no one could understand me. I felt really frightened. I didn't know why I'd been sent back or what my mission was. After an experience like that you'd expect everything in your life to suddenly become clear and get put into perspective, but instead I just felt more muddled and confused. By day, I went through the motions at the City firm where I worked as an accounts manager, but at night I'd slump into a fog of depression.

I rang the hospital for my medical records, but was told they had been 'lost'. I was distraught. What happened to me had been so traumatic and yet it was as if, for the rest of the world, it had ceased to exist.

Luckily I was in touch with the anaesthetist and he sneaked out a copy of my records for me. Obviously they weren't quite as 'lost' as they'd seemed! I still have those records. I don't know what I'm going to do with them, or why it was so important for me to get them, but I'm glad I know they're safe.

Gradually, agonisingly slowly, I began to pull myself out of the pit I'd been in since the operation and regain some control of my life. Being blasted with so much histamine had all but wiped out my immune system, leaving me allergic to loads of things, so I had to attend a specialist allergy clinic to try to build up some resistance.

But the experience also left me with another, more unexpected legacy. Like I said, I've always been a bit psychic, but after leaving the hospital my premonitions were just going crazy. It was stupid little things, like I went out for a drink one night and met this bloke – no one special, just someone I chatted to for a few minutes. Then a few days later I was at my boss's barbecue and I said to my friend, 'In a few minutes, that bloke we met the other night is going to walk in,' and sure enough in he came. That's what I mean about it being stupid little things. It would have been all right if it was earth-shattering revelations, but this just made me think I was going bonkers.

I'd also kind of lose myself in space and time. I know you're probably thinking at this point 'crazy', but there's no other way to explain it. Like one time I was skiing down a mountain with my sister and she looked back and I'd totally disappeared. It sounds mad but I felt myself fall into a different dimension. Just for a few seconds and then I was back again. I've since met other people who do this, so I know I haven't completely lost it.

Four years after the operation, I had a child, my lovely son Dom. Though I'm now divorced from his father, becoming a mother was something I never thought would happen to me, and it has changed my life completely. I became a lot more chilled and, to my relief, the bombardment of premonitions slowed to a manageable trickle.

Buoyed up by my new responsibilities as a mother, I took the big brave step of going freelance, starting up my own business-coaching company, which is something I'd never have had the guts to do without my son to inspire me.

In recent months, I've also met a lovely man who I love to bits and who makes me very happy.

But, in many ways, life since the operation has been like one step forward, two steps back. For every fantastic event, there have been two that have set my world reeling again. My best friend's husband and my brother-in-law both died. Relations with Dom's father have been very strained, and there have been times when I really have questioned what I'm doing here.

There have been many occasions where I've wondered why I got sent back and what on earth my task could be. It's very frustrating. When my life seems like it's in a downward spiral, I find myself talking out loud to 'God' or whatever that panel was I found myself in front of.

'Why did I have to come back?' I ask. 'What makes me so special? You have a sick sense of humour to have sent me back to this.'

I just wish I knew what my task is supposed to be. I keep asking for signs, but I've never had any clear instructions. I've been to see psychics and have been told that it will all become clearer as time goes on, but, ten years after the operation, I'm still waiting for all to be revealed.

Sometimes I read other accounts from people who've 'died' and come back but they all seem so positive compared to mine. I find myself thinking, 'Why was I given a different experience to everyone else?'

But, you know, life goes on. I have to be strong for my son and I have to believe that everything that I've been through has happened for a reason. I just don't know what it is yet.

In the meantime, I'll keep finding out as much as I can about spiritualism. I hope that doesn't make me sound studious and pompous – I drink, I smoke, I'm a party person, but I'm also a spiritual person. The two can co-exist! And I'll keep looking out for new opportunities and openings that might make my journey clearer.

At the end of the day, I don't want to be labelled as the girl who 'died', but as the girl who knew how to live.

# 3

## BRIAN SCHMIDT, 42
### POLICEMAN AND FIREFIGHTER, MISSOURI, USA

STANDING IN THE church at the funeral of my friend, Susan, I couldn't stop the tears from running down my face. I was wiping them away with the back of my hand, but still they came, just as they had at the funeral of our other best friend Lisa just days before.

Susan and Lisa had been killed in the same car accident and their deaths had totally slain me. For the past few years, we'd been inseparable, the Three Fusiliers, one for all and all for one. Now there was just me.

As I watched the coffin being carried out of the church, I made two vows to these girls, my two fellow Fusiliers. I vowed that I would never forget them, that I would take their memories with me to the grave. And I also vowed that, when my time came to die, I'd make sure it was these two girls who came to meet me.

Six years later, that's exactly what happened.

My 'death' happened seventeen years ago, but the events are more real to me and more vivid than anything that has happened since.

It was a Sunday in mid-April 1989 and I was travelling back from a sales show to the small rented house in Mexico, Missouri, which I shared with my wife of two years. I was a speciality-foods salesman at that time, travelling a regular sales route, selling over 6,000 speciality-food items to grocery stores, restaurants and health-food stores. I'd been working for that company for about one and a half years. I was twenty-six years old, making good money and enjoying my life. I dreamed of becoming sales manager for the entire district, which would put me in charge of all the other salespersons. Isn't it funny how your priorities can change so much? Now when I look back on that person with his goals and aspirations, it seems like someone else.

As I drove home on this particular spring day, I was thinking how beautiful it was with the leaves beginning to show green on the trees after the harsh winter. The weather was perfect – clear, with temperatures of around 75 degrees or so. I was driving northbound on a double-lane divided highway. On the radio was a really great song (although I have never since been able to remember what the song was), and I was happy to be going home finally after having to give up my weekend to work at the trade show.

I'd had to miss out on a good friend's wedding that weekend. He'd asked me to be his best man, but my boss had refused to give me the time off. I was disappointed at missing the wedding and not getting to see my friend, but he was never far from my mind during that day. As I was driving, I was guessing that he'd be at the reception about now and wondering how the service had gone.

All of a sudden I became aware of a car approaching the highway from the west on a gravel road. Out of the corner of my eye, I saw the car cross the southbound lanes of traffic and drive through the central section, approaching the stop sign where traffic waiting to cross was supposed to pull up, before continuing across the northbound lanes of traffic.

Looking back, I realised that the car had never stopped at the stop sign before driving across the southbound lanes of traffic, but at the time I hadn't really taken this in. Then, instead of stopping at the stop sign in the middle section, the car continued straight across the northbound lanes of traffic, directly into the path of my car.

Isn't it strange how your perceptions change when you're under that sort of stress? My mind saw the car as a mid-seventies Lincoln, huge compared to the compact car I was driving. But in fact it turned out to be a mid-sized mid-eighties Oldsmobile. The only explanation I can give for the mistake is that the car was so close, looming so large in my vision, that my mind changed it to a big model.

I did, however, get the colour correct. It was green.

The car was being driven by an elderly man, with his elderly wife in the passenger seat. They didn't survive the crash, so no one will ever know what caused them to plough through two stop signs like that, but their faces will always remain etched on to my mind, frozen in that one moment which linked us inextricably together.

Everything went into slow motion. The events of the crash couldn't have taken more than a few moments, yet every little detail, every fleeting thought, remains indelibly branded into my memory, as if it unfolded over the course of several hours, rather than seconds.

I said or thought an expletive. I still believe that I said it, but, considering how fast everything happened, maybe it just flitted across my mind.

I recall that my right hand pulled the gearshift backward – it was an automatic but, like most American cars, that movement will make the car's transmission shift to a lower gear and help slow the car down. The green car was travelling from my left to my right, so, at the same time, I turned the steering wheel hard left. I remember thinking, 'If I can just hit this car in the rear axle, it will spin the car on the front axle out of my way, and maybe we can all live through this thing.'

There seemed to be no sound other than the wind. I recall thinking, 'That's really weird, where's the wind coming from?'

Suddenly it struck me: 'Okay, there isn't going to be any sound until the cars hit.' Then I wondered why my car wasn't turning. I had turned the wheel hard left with my hand, but nothing happened. As the cars drew closer together, I realised I'd reached a point where there was absolutely nothing I could do to affect the outcome of this event. I was just there and it was going to happen all around me. That was the first time in my life – and the last, come to think of it – that I'd felt so completely helpless.

I watched the people in the other car getting closer and closer, at first a few feet, then just inches. The man was looking forward through the windshield, the woman was turned slightly towards him and I believed talking to him. She held what I thought was a small transistor radio in her right hand near her right ear. I thought, 'I haven't seen a radio like that since about 1971 or so.' Then contact was made and, sure enough, I heard the sound of the impact, and then the view of the other people was immediately obscured by steam from the burst radiator of my car. I remember knowing that's what it was. Then my car began to spin slowly towards the west. I couldn't see at all because of the steam and I remember thinking, 'All I need now is for a great big articulated truck to plough into us as well!'

Then I reasoned that, if the wind was coming from the west and my car was spinning from north to west, we'd soon spin to a point where the steam would be blowing away from the car and wouldn't be blocking my vision. Sure enough, when the car spun facing the southwest, the steam was carried out of my field of view and I could see down the highway from the direction in which I had just come. I remember thinking again, 'Man, am I lucky there isn't a truck bearing down on us!' Then my car stopped.

Realising that my car had stopped moving, I thought, 'I've got to get out of here!' Then I remember my head bowing and my chin striking my chest and there being a big 'phooofing' sound. (The only way I can describe that sound, it's like that made when you lock your lower lip behind your upper teeth and blow your lip back out into normal position... phooofing). I recall feeling like I was phooofed, like I was a drop of liquid being quickly forced through a straw. I heard and *felt* the phooofing.

Next thing, I was out of the car, 'standing' (for want of a better word) next to the driver's door. I knew, without being at all alarmed by this knowledge, that I was out of my body. I felt I had a 'form', a vague awareness of arms and legs and height, but I also had an indescribable feeling of ultimate freedom, a feeling of freedom stronger than anything you can imagine.

I looked down at the guy sitting in the driver's seat and thought, 'Hey, that's me, and I'm sort of a mess. Not too bad, though, it doesn't look like anything was torn off the body; it all looks pretty much there, but it is dead.' I had worked in a funeral home for about a year and a half and was quite familiar with dead bodies.

At this moment, I heard a voice behind me and turned. There, 'standing' (again for want of a better term) were those two friends, Lisa and Susan, who had been killed in that car wreck in 1983.

I'd become friends with the two of them in September of 1981, my first year at college. From the start we were inseparable. We were known amongst ourselves as 'the Three Fusiliers'. Lisa was my best friend. There were no secrets between us. I knew she hadn't had an easy life and she never seemed totally comfortable in her skin. It was Lisa who introduced me to Susan. Susan was a wild child. There wasn't anything that she wouldn't do once, and she claimed a history of juvenile delinquency which I never doubted. Incredibly, she had eight sisters. She was petite, with blonde hair and a limitless energy and enthusiasm for life which was impossible not to love.

I'd known them both for two years when they were killed. They were together (of course) and travelling to another state to see a guy. I was supposed to be going with them, but had to work at the last minute. That was the period I was working at a funeral home to try to make a bit of money to stay in school. My mother was ill with the cancer that eventually killed her, so money was tight. Lisa and Susan were travelling in Susan's car when they turned the wrong way on a four-lane divided highway and crashed head-on into a truck at the crest of a hill.

I can't describe what an impact their deaths had on me. In one sense I could reason that for Lisa, who'd always had such a hard time adjusting to the world, death might come as some sort of a relief. I was sad, of course, but I could convince myself she would be happy to be finally out of this life. But it was Susan that I cried for. I think I cried non-stop for two days. I cried until my stomach hurt, my eyes were sore and my heart was torn. I still miss her terribly.

I went to both funerals, the last Fusilier, vowing to take their memories to my grave. I swore to myself that, when my time came, I would really like to have those two girls come to collect me (if that was how it was done). Well, here they were.

Looking back on it, the amazing thing was that I wasn't surprised in the least to see them there. I remember saying, or at least transmitting the message: 'Hey, Lisa, Hey, Susan' in a nonchalant manner, as though I had just met them in the Student Union after a break in classes or having lost track of them in a grocery store. I began to tell Lisa about my body. I said, 'Hey, Lisa, get a load of this,' and nodded towards myself seated in the car as if I was sort of amused by the situation.

The sense of sheer exhilarating freedom I felt being 'out' of my body was overwhelming. It occurred to me that, in my current state, I could do anything I wanted. I could go anywhere and no laws of physics could stop me. I realised I could even go to the Eiffel Tower if I wanted. Weirdly, that's the exact place that came to mind, even though I'd never before had any yearning to visit the Eiffel Tower or any thoughts about it at all, other than maybe to answer a question on a fifth-grade geography class quiz. I began to revel in my current feeling, a feeling of such wellbeing that even now, nearly two decades on, I still miss it.

Lisa said, 'Brian, you must listen closely.' (Did she say there isn't much time or was that just information implied through thought?) Then she went on, 'You must look', and she pointed or rather directed my attention in some other manner (it's hard to describe exactly *how* talking, moving, standing was done throughout the experience – it just was) to the western horizon. I noticed that pretty much all the world was muted, like a television that isn't getting good reception – occasionally the black and white is broken by a blob of colour, but pretty much it's black and white. In the sky, however, was my life. It was like seeing it on a movie screen (widescreen), in colour, on a VCR that's stuck in fast-forward. But, rather than seeing it only, I was *feeling* it like I was in the life and 'standing' with Lisa and Susan at the same time. The life played literally from my birth to my 'death'.

I saw my mother giving birth to me. I got to watch myself grow and play as a small child. I saw myself running my pedal car into the door facings in our hallway and getting banished to the garage with it. I later found the mark on the door trim where my car had hit. I got to experience everything that had happened to me – all in ultra-fast-forward time, and yet slow enough for me to relive every moment. I watched my relationships with my family and understood that I and my sister were born of these people because we needed the experiences that we had and we were all together for a reason. I watched myself grow and realised that my relationship with my grandfather had been especially essential in my life. Fishing trips with him really stood out at me as especially enjoyable. I lived through my mother's illness and ultimate death, and noted that the whole event was educational for both of us.

I went all the way through to marriage and even got a glimpse into the future. I saw my wife getting news that I had been killed. I saw her crying. I remember thinking, 'Oh, I don't want her to cry and be sad.' But at the same time I got the message: 'Everything that happens to us affects all others, and those it affects are supposed to be affected. It is for their own good and they must experience it.' I think it was Lisa that told me that but I can't be certain; I was still concentrating on the life 'screen' in the sky. Through all the things that happened, good and bad, I didn't feel judged in any way. I was not left with anyone telling me, 'You sinned! You're a sinner!' Rather I was left to form an opinion of the life, but not in terms of whether I'd been a good person or a bad person. When I was finished seeing/living all the various scenes, my immediate thought was: 'That was a good life.' I was matter-of-fact about it, as if I was affectionately commenting on a well-cooked steak that I'd enjoyed eating.

I got the feeling at that particular moment that there had been previous lives and when these were completed I'd gone through identical or similar reviews. But I wasn't curious about these other lives. They were done and I'd completed them, leaving them of no further consequence. I also understood that this life would be of no consequence now that it was done.

At that point, I realised that all the answers to any questions I had were contained within me. In that sense, I knew everything. I had all knowledge inside myself. If a question began formulating in my mind, the complete and expanded answer and how it related to all other information and answers came to me before the question was even really started. All information that I sought was instantly mine to analyse, and all information that related to that information was also mine to analyse. I know it sounds bizarre but it was like all knowledge was at my fingertips and instantly in my mind.

I knew, without knowing how, that this was my actual state of being – not the human body I'd occupied until then. I was a creature/being as I now found myself who had, for some time, used the lifeless piece of meat inside the car. I did feel kind of sad for my body though. Now it wasn't any further use, it sort of seemed like a waste, and it had performed well for me. It was like the feeling you get when you trade in a much-loved car.

All of this didn't seem to take long – in our time, a period of about twenty seconds or so. Everything that occurred to me and happened did so within that fleeting amount of time.

Then Lisa said, or rather communicated, 'You must listen.' There was urgency in her words. 'You have accomplished enough that you can go with us –' here she paused '– or you can stay. But if you stay we have to know why and you have to tell us. Also, you must know this: if you stay, it's going to be very, very hard.'

I knew Lisa meant that I had accomplished what I had come to the physical world to do and learn. There was some goal in my coming (I don't remember what exactly), and I'd achieved enough of what I was supposed to do and learn to move on. I was free to leave. But, to my surprise, I found myself saying flatly, 'I have to stay.'

Lisa asked, 'Why?'

Again I was surprised to find myself stating, 'I don't have any children yet.'

I had never given children much thought before the accident. When I said, 'I don't have children yet', it wasn't because I had a huge yearning to produce them, it was rather because that was another marker in my life experience that hadn't been met yet. I didn't feel emotional about it. It was rather like I'd finally got round to painting my house but then it had started to rain and I was telling someone that I still needed another day to paint around the windows.

I was aware that Susan had said nothing during all of this. It was only Lisa doing the talking. Then I became aware that, beyond Susan, there was 'someone' else. I realised that this 'person' was listening intently and that I was not allowed to see him or her.

It's hard to explain it, but this 'person' appeared only as a huge presence that was perceivable as waves of distortion, shielded from my consciousness so that I could not see him or her directly. There's a Schwarzenegger film called *Predator* which features a 'cloaked' alien, and this is the type of effect I saw. Not that I felt threatened at all. There were no feelings of danger, only a realisation through this visual distortion of a nearby 'presence'.

Lisa said, 'All right, you have to know that your heart stopped when you hit the steering wheel, but you will not have permanent injury from this. Your injuries will be a broken sternum, a cut on your finger and you'll lose a couple of teeth.'

I said, 'Okay' and heard that phooof again. Then everything was black. At first I was confused and couldn't figure out exactly where I was. Then I heard a sound, like a far-off boom. There was then silence and then another boom, then another, then another closer together. Then I heard a heartbeat sound and another and realised that the booming was my heart starting.

I remember thinking, 'Why, that's my heart starting!' Then the realisation hit me that I needed a breath of air really, really badly, like I imagine the feeling you get when you're deep under water and you're desperately trying to get to the surface but you realise you're going to run out of air before you get there. So I took the longest, deepest gasping breath that I can ever recall taking. When it was finished, I opened my eyes and observed the scene.

I don't know exactly how long I was in the car before help arrived, but it was a long time. I have always believed that I was in the car for about forty-five minutes to an hour before anyone figured out I was alive and got me out. But it's really hard to estimate time when you've just come back from someplace where there is no time and you're operating outside of those boundaries. It's also hard to estimate time when you're hurt.

After coming back to consciousness, I immediately looked at my left hand. There was a cut on my hand and I observed that it wasn't bleeding. I noticed that the blood vessels in the back of my hand, which are normally very visible and prominent, were not standing up like normal. I saw the veins suddenly swelling as blood pressure increased and then the cut began bleeding.

I picked the rear-view mirror out of the seat next to me (passenger side), and examined my teeth – I've always had a thing about my teeth, so weirdly they were my first concern. I observed that I had indeed damaged my teeth just as Lisa said. The top of the steering wheel had punched me in the mouth at the same time it drove through my sternum. Bear in mind that this whole time I was squashed into a little area with the steering wheel pinning me to the seat, the top of the car crushed down, the floor-board pushed up and my knees ten inches through the dashboard. I knew that my chest was hurt as Lisa had told me my sternum would be broken, and it hurt very badly to breathe.

I checked my femurs. I knew from working in the funeral home that the femurs are always broken in this type of accident. Mine weren't which is a miracle unto itself. I was amazed that so far Lisa had been one hundred per cent spot on. I didn't know at this time about the nerve damage in my legs which, although minor, would never quite heal.

I looked at the steering wheel, while trying to get some space between it and the seat, and noticed that the cover in the centre was broken and gone. Through the hole, there was the screw portion of a half-inch bolt with a nut on it. The bolt end stuck out about two inches from the base of the steering wheel and it was this that had skewered me in the chest. I still have a dent in the sternum where it went in. It's one of the few physical reminders — well, that and the constant popping and cracking noises my chest makes.

About this time the lady in the other car regained consciousness. I don't like to talk about that portion of the experience because I was trapped in my car and I had to listen to that woman die. Bear in mind that my knees were through the dash, the top was crumpled down on top of me and all the doors were jammed shut. Add the steering wheel pinning me to my seat and the fact I couldn't talk and you can see why I was sort of a captive audience to the event. I tried to free myself to help her but couldn't do it. She was the passenger, the driver never regained consciousness, which is probably a good thing for him, and I had to listen to her dying slowly and painfully. I used to re-experience that in my dreams every night, but thankfully I haven't for a while.

After that I went to a kind of 'black place'; I suppose I drifted in and out of consciousness. Periodically I'd hear sirens or people talking, but I couldn't speak.

I heard a guy who I found out later was a paramedic telling people, 'This one's gone!' Apparently, he'd felt my neck and couldn't find a pulse. I don't know why that is, as I wasn't 'dead' at this point; I had already come back from wherever I'd been. I was just in the black place. There were more sirens, and the sound of power tools. I heard people giving directions to others. I deduced that those noises were a fire-fighter rescue team cutting the other car to get the people out because I could hear the metal on the car popping.

I became aware that someone was standing just outside the door of my car, driver's side. I heard his clothes moving, his feet shifting and scuffing on the pavement, and the sound of him writing. I heard this guy shout to someone, 'You said this one is dead, right?' I heard the paramedic yell, 'Yeah, he's gone!' and then the guy next to me began writing again.

I thought, 'Hey, I'm not dead. I better show them that pretty quick, or they're going to leave me in here.' I made a concentrated effort to take a deeper breath, although it was incredibly painful (breathing with a fractured sternum is pure torture so you do it as shallowly as possible). Concentrating all my efforts, I pulled myself up from the black place, raised my head and saw a uniform-clad Missouri State Trooper standing next to me. (This is the statewide police agency responsible for safety and enforcement on US highways.)

The trooper was bent over trying to see the vehicle

identification number of my car. The VIN is a unique number assigned to every car made in the US. It is a sixteen-digit number set into the left side of the dashboard next to the driver's side. This guy was trying to read the number through the windshield but, as my hand had crushed the glass, it made it difficult to read and he was really focusing hard.

After taking that long painful breath, I managed finally to make a sound. Stunned, the trooper looked up at me, his eyes huge and round with surprise. He started making a series of nonsensical noises, so shocked he was momentarily unable to find words. Then he yelled, 'Hey, this one's alive!'

He started telling me that he didn't know who I was and asking if I knew who I was. I was nodding as much as I could and he kept asking me questions, then demanding to know why I wasn't answering. He kept questioning and questioning but I was in no state to answer. I noticed my cheque book was embedded in the passenger side of the dashboard. I reached over and pulled it free of the crack it had made when it struck. I handed the trooper the cheque book which contained all my identification details.

'What's this for?' he asked me blankly.

'Name, address,' I croaked quietly. Then I drifted back to the black place.

Some time afterwards, I became aware that the paramedic from earlier was reaching through the wreckage, asking me questions and checking such things as pulse and skin temperature, and trying to assess my injuries. I told him exactly what Lisa had said was wrong with me – broken sternum, damaged teeth, cuts – and that I was going to have nerve damage in my legs. I remember that he responded with 'Oookkkaaaayyy', like he thought I'd lost the plot.

Then the fire rescue crew came over to my car and started cutting. The other people had already been removed by this time and I believe had both been taken to hospital.

The paramedic talked to me while they were cutting. I remember that he kept telling me, 'Stay with me, man, stay with me!' He said that they were going to totally immobilise me to keep from injuring me further when they moved me. I tried to explain that I wasn't seriously injured and to just 'get me out of here and throw me on a stretcher.'

'How do you know? Are you a doctor?' he asked me.

I remember telling him, 'I know because Lisa told me what was wrong with me.'

He didn't ask any more questions but they did totally immobilise me before removing me from the car. I kept arguing and telling them what was wrong with me but, of course, they didn't take my word for it. As they were cutting me out and the paramedic was speaking, I was still passing in and out of consciousness.

Carried out of the car, I became aware of television cameras at the scene from a local news crew that had been notified about the crash. I remember saying, 'Get that f★★★★★★ camera out of my face.'

Then I was in an ambulance with a female paramedic sitting on a bench next to me. I remember asking her, 'Where exactly are we?'

She said, 'You're in an ambulance'.

I said, 'No, where exactly on the *road* are we? How far from the city?'

She replied, 'I'm afraid I have no way of knowing, there's only a little window.'

Then, as if it was the most normal thing in the world, I remember saying, 'That's all right, I'll go out and look.' And I passed right through the side of the ambulance. Weirdly, I wasn't at all surprised that I'd done that – it was something that happened at will. At the time, I knew that it was something that I'd always be able to do and that it was a natural occurrence. Of course, it hadn't happened before, and hasn't happened since, although I like to think I might some day remember how I did it. Once outside the ambulance, I could see a rock quarry that I always used as a landmark and I noted that we were almost to it. After going back through the side of the ambulance, I told her, 'We're almost to the rock quarry. Good, we're getting close.'

Stunned, the paramedic got up and went to look through a small window on the side of the ambulance. 'Oh, I see it, yes,' she said, 'but how…?' She didn't finish that sentence, nor did she say anything else other than, 'You just lie quiet, we're almost there', when she sat back down. Then she moved a little away from me and sat looking at me with a strange look on her face.

I was in the hospital for just twenty-four hours. The doctors were afraid that I had bruised my heart in the accident so they kept me hooked up to machines all night. I didn't talk to anyone in the hospital about what had happened to me. I wasn't sure how to bring it up. Everyone in the hospital kept looking at me like they didn't know what to do with me. They looked at me like I shouldn't have been there and like *they* didn't know what to say. It was a very uncomfortable night. The worst thing was not being able to sleep. Every time I started to doze off, I could feel myself begin to float out of my body and I thought I was 'dying' again, but knew I was supposed to stay, so I would wake myself up.

Later, in the ER, two strange things happened. First, the paramedic who'd checked me inside the car came to see me. 'You look much better than you did a while ago,' he joked. I told him I felt better. Then he looked more serious and told me he'd believed I was dead after checking my pulse and not finding one. I think he missed it because he didn't get there until after I was back in my body and was in the dark place where I could hear but I couldn't react. My heart had started beating again by that time. 'In all the years I've been doing this, I've never checked anyone and been mistaken about them being living or dead, until now,' he said.

I told him, 'Who says you were mistaken?'

He stared at me, but then a big grin spread over his face. 'You be cool, man,' he told me, and then left.

The second thing was that a nurse asked me what medical training I'd had. Apparently, I'd told people both at the scene of the crash and in the ER that I had a broken sternum and a cut on my finger, and that I would lose two teeth. She was puzzled when I told her that I was not in the medical profession, nor had I ever had any training.

My wife, Tina, had been told about the accident in a telephone call. When she turned up at the hospital, she was in a real state as they'd refused to give her any details over the phone, and she'd immediately thought the worst. 'I thought you were dead,' she cried when she saw me. At that time I didn't want to make things worse by telling her I had actually been dead – and come back. It's one of the great sadnesses of my life that, when I did get round to telling her, she couldn't accept it. 'That didn't happen,' she told me, refusing to talk about it further. In time, I stopped bringing it up and she, relieved that I was 'over all that', stopped treating me like an alien.

60

In time, I mostly recovered from my injuries. I say 'mostly' because my broken sternum has never really healed – it pops and cracks in quite an off-putting way – and I have nerve damage in my legs. It's only a skin-surface thing but I get false nervous transmissions from time to time. I'll brush against something and feel extreme heat when I should feel pressure. Sometimes if feels as though there's a thousand baby spiders crawling up the front of my thighs – that sort of thing. Also, I lost two of my front teeth. They didn't fall out, but the impact of the steering wheel killed them and they had to be root-canalled.

I've since read other near-death experiences where people have said that they felt angry at being made to return to life. That was never the case with me. I knew I had returned because it was my choice to return. I could not be angry about my choice. I knew that I had to go on in this life because I wasn't done and was resigned to doing so. I knew it was important to carry on, although I was rather apprehensive because Lisa had told me that it would be 'very, very hard'. That was running around and around in my head because I was trying to picture what 'hard' things lay ahead of me.

Now I know the reason we're here – to gain knowledge and experience for our other existence. I know that there's a predetermined pattern for all life everywhere from the smallest microbe to space. What I don't know is why I'm here, specifically, whether there's more in store for me.

When I think back on being in that other state and remember what it felt like, I do sometimes miss it, but I know that someday I'll be back there again. But, for now, I'm supposed to be here. I chose to come back. I'll return when it's my time and, in the meantime, I still have the memory.

Certainly, I've made enormous life changes as a result of the experience. I left the food company because I felt I needed to do something that contributed to the world rather than taking from it. For a year or so, I messed around restoring cars with a friend and then I joined the police department where I'm now a lieutenant and a part-time fire-fighter (it's normal to have those two roles in law enforcement here). My entire life has turned around. I just know it's where I should be and I'm doing what I should be doing. It is my job to force others to be aware of the things that they need to work on in their lives. I'm usually their last stop. By the time they run into me and I get them into court, they've already ignored countless warnings from other sources. I like what I do. I'm good at it.

My wife and I went on to have two children, just as I knew I would, who are now fourteen and ten. I've never told them about my experience or that I came back for them. What kid wants to be lumbered with knowledge like that? I've always made a real effort to stay home with my kids as much as possible and think of fun things to do with them.

I know that some people find religion in a big way after a near-death experience, but I've never really thought of myself as particularly religious. I was brought up a Methodist but always had the attitude that God probably knew who I was but we didn't speak all that regularly. When my mother died in 1983 after her long fight with ovarian cancer, I was left feeling adrift spiritually, but, since my car crash, my spiritual connections to other people have intensified greatly. I've found myself to be much more emotional after this experience, and I feel other people's emotional pain. I'm certainly not afraid of dying any more. Life is clear now and there's purpose to all things.

I haven't told anyone in my job about my experience – I don't think they'd understand. There really aren't any words that can describe the experience exactly. How does one go about explaining the unexplainable? In fact, I've told very few people – unless I think it'll actually do some good.

One time, a few years after the crash, I ran into a good friend of mine who told me about a worrying dream his mother had had. He was a plumber and his mum had dreamed that he'd been killed in a trench collapse. I found myself telling him about my experience, and how it had made me unafraid of dying and I know he felt reassured by the time we parted. Just three days later he was killed – when a trench collapsed, just as his mother had predicted.

When I heard about his death, of course I was sad that I wouldn't see him again, but I knew it wasn't an accident that I had run into him that day and related my story to him. As time went on, I found out that, in his last week of life, he had run into everyone who had ever been important in his life, friend and foe. He had buried the hatchet with all those with whom he had problems and, I think, said goodbye to all his friends.

I don't really like the term 'near-death experience'. What happened to me wasn't 'near death', it was a return from death. But I guess human beings are always going to want labels – and labels are nearly always inadequate.

When Lisa told me life was going to be 'hard', I worried that she was hinting that my next death would be a horrible, lingering, painful type of thing. I was worried I was going to get cancer or something like that. But now I think she was talking about life here – that it's harder than life in that other post-life state. When you've experienced the blissful freedom of that other state, the human body can feel like a burden. It feels like you're weighed down, like you're trying to move in a pair of mud-laden wet overalls – and that takes a lot of adjusting to. But it's worth it, because now I have the knowledge of what's coming. I *know* that eternity exists, because I've seen it. Best of all, I know what it feels like to come 'home' – I can't wait to be there again.

# 4

# JANET LARSEN, 55

## NURSE, WHITBY

IF SOMEONE TOLD me today, 'Janet, you're dying of cancer,' I'd answer, 'Thank God for that.' You see, I know there's nothing to fear from death. Nothing at all. And I should know – I've been there once and I've been trying to get back there ever since.

I'm fifty-five now, and all this happened when I was seventeen, so it was a long time ago. And yet it's still so clear in my head.

I've suffered from diabetes since being a small child. In those days, much less was known about it than is known now, especially where I grew up (and still live), near Whitby in Yorkshire. Anyhow, by the time I was seventeen, I'd learned to manage my condition pretty well and I was, in most respects, a perfectly normal teenager, riding horses and going on dates, all the usual stuff.

This particular day, my dear old dad had waltzed in with a German sausage, which was pretty exotic for the time.

'It smells a bit funny, Dad,' I said, sniffing.

'Nonsense,' he said. 'Give it a try.'

Of course, I did and almost immediately started vomiting. The problem with me is, once I start, it's almost impossible for me to stop. I was sick until I couldn't be sick any more and then I lay on the sofa snuggled weakly under a blanket.

My mum and dad were due to go out to a council function, but my mum was worried about leaving me.

'I'll be fine,' I told them.

But I wasn't. Not long after they'd gone out, I started getting terrible pains in my chest. It really hurt to draw breath. I was in agony.

I remember needing the bathroom and doing my best to crawl up the stairs. When I started out, the clock at the bottom said 7pm but by the time I got up there it was ten past nine – that's how hard it was to get up those twelve small steps!

When I came downstairs again, I managed to crawl back to the sofa. Everything hurt. The pain in my chest was crowding everything else out. All I could think about was fighting the pain to get enough air to breathe.

At some point I became aware of my parents coming home, but, though I could hear them, I couldn't speak. My mum took one look at me and screamed. Later she told me I looked like a 'dried-up Egyptian mummy' as I'd lost so much fluid from my body. I imagine it's like when a tissue that was once wet is left to dry and shrivel.

My parents called out the local doctor, who arrived soon after. He was a young doctor who had been studying new methods of treating diabetes. He gave me a massive shot of insulin, but his prognosis was grim. 'I'm afraid this girl won't survive until the ambulance gets here,' he told my shocked parents, not imagining for a minute that I could hear him. 'Her breathing has almost stopped. She has about eight minutes left – ten at the most.'

Immediately, my dad sprang into action, racing out to get his car and bring it to the front door. My mother lifted me up in her arms and bundled me into the back seat with the doctor following behind in his own car. Typically, as my father sped through the darkened streets towards the hospital, he was flagged down by a police car.

'Do you realise the speed you're going, sir?' the policeman began.

But my father cut him off before he could go any further. 'My daughter's in the back. She's dying,' he shouted.

The policeman shone a torch into my face. What he saw so shocked him that he waved my dad on and jumped into his own car to give us a police escort.

At the hospital, staff were waiting with equipment to meet the car. But, by the time I arrived, the insulin had done its job and the crippling pain had eased. I was feeling more and more peaceful, although all around me the fight was still on to save my life.

I must have passed out then but at some point later I was put on a bed in a darkened ward. I know there was a nurse stroking my forehead for a while, but in time she went elsewhere and I was alone. I've always had a fear of darkness, which is with me to this day, but for some reason this particular darkness didn't bother me. I allowed myself to drift in it.

Then the darkness became a tunnel and I was drifting through it towards this incredible light at the end. There was no pain, no stress, only the darkness and this amazing light. Oh, I wish I could describe the light – how wonderful it was, but there are no words for it.

It wasn't coming towards me; I was travelling towards it. I was drifting so blissfully, it was beautiful.

Then my journey was interrupted by the doctors arriving back at my bed and turning on the overhead light. I was upset because I didn't want that light. I wanted the other light, the beautiful light. But I couldn't see it because my blissful dark tunnel was all lit up by this artificial light.

The doctors were trying to make me talk, but I wasn't concentrating on them. I was trying to get back to that feeling of peace.

'We have to see how much urine you pass,' one of them told me. 'This catheter may feel uncomfortable.'

I felt a slight touch, but by that stage I didn't care because the tunnel was back and my lovely beautiful light had returned and I was going towards it.

Then I really did pass out. The next thing I remember was my nose twitching and the most delicious smell of bacon wafting over me. 'I could murder a bacon butty,' I said, my eyes still shut.

When I finally opened them, there was a nurse standing next to me with her hand over her mouth, crying. 'I'll go and get the doctor,' she gasped.

I couldn't understand what was going on, or why the other women in the ward were staring and smiling and looking so happy. It was only later that I learned I'd been in a coma for nine whole days and had nearly died on several occasions. During that time I'd had someone watching over me twenty-four hours a day. Being the youngest person on the ward, they'd all become protective of me during those days.

'You looked like an angel, lying there so still,' one of them told me.

No wonder the poor nurse had been so shocked when I suddenly asked for bacon!

After that I quickly recovered, though I've never quite got over losing nine entire days from my life. My NDE left me changed in many fundamental ways.

Before then, I'd been doing a bit of this and a bit of that, not really sure what I wanted to do with my life. But, after my coma, I knew what I was supposed to do. Nursing. I trained as a nurse and worked in that field for many years before joining up with the merchant navy so that I could see something of the world. Even after the navy, though, I went back to nursing, specialising in hospice work.

Working at the hospice brings you into contact with many dying people. I've been able to help them by telling them what happened to me and how peaceful it was, and in return I've been lucky enough to share some truly beautiful moments. Some people have talked to me as they died, seeing the light and telling me, 'It's beautiful.' Others, I know, have seen loved ones in the light. 'I'm coming,' they've said to these waiting spirits. 'Hold on, I'm coming.'

When it was my dad's time to go, I sat with him as he died.

'Can you see anything?' I asked him.

'Lines,' he told me.

'Go along with them,' I told him. 'Go with the lines.'

Then he muttered just one word, 'peaceful', and he was gone.

Years later, I was the one to switch off my mother's life-support machine. I didn't want anyone else to do it.

Perhaps the most amazing death scene occurred while I was

still in hospital recovering from my coma. I'd become really friendly with a lady in a neighbouring bed. As she was paralysed from the neck down and couldn't move, her only release was talking and I'd sit and chat with her for hours.

One night I looked over to her bed and was amazed to see her sit up and hold her arms out in front of her. It was funny the angle she was holding them out – not straight in front, but slightly upwards towards something high up at the end of her bed.

Being young and naive as I was, I thought, 'Oh, how fantastic, she's got better!'

Then the nurses were all around her and screens went up and there was nothing else to see.

I dozed off to sleep and when I woke up her bed was empty.

'We've taken her to another ward,' the nurses told me, trying to soften the blow. But later it came out she'd actually died. They needn't have lied to me. I know she was at peace when she died. Can you imagine a more incredible freedom than being able to sit up again after years of not being able to move?

The feeling of utter joyfulness I found in that light I saw only once when I was seventeen has never left me. Throughout my life, even in the worst times, I've known that I'm not really alone and that peace is the reward for death. So, years later, when I contracted the MRSA bug in hospital and had to have my leg amputated, I was philosophical about it. I knew I'd get through it and, if I didn't, I knew that was fine too.

I've had a good life. I married a Norwegian man thirty-five years ago and we've had three children and seven grandchildren. My family makes me incredibly happy. And yet, if someone were to tell me I was going to die tomorrow, I wouldn't mind at all.

Death is nothing to be afraid of. I think of it as just passing into a different time dimension. You know when you get that feeling of déjà vu, like something has happened before. Well, I believe that's just a time-slip. And I believe that's all death is too.

We don't ever just disappear. We're always around, even after death, although obviously not in the same body.

I often joke that, when I die, I want to come back as one of those little Japanese toy dogs – they lead the life of luxury!

Death is just the beginning.

# 5

## RENÉ TURNER, 59

### CAMPAIGNER, NEW ZEALAND

IT'S FUNNY HOW some things are always 'known' and can't be changed. My mum has shown me an entry from her diary written when I was just five years old which reads: 'This child pronounced she would never marry and would die when she was thirty-five, and would never give me grandchildren.'

I have never married, nor have I had children. And, when I was one month past my thirty-fifth birthday, I died.

It was 24 February 1982. I was with Miles, my partner of four years, and we were driving back home from the optical-instrument-repair business I'd set up in Newcastle, Australia.

I'm from England originally. I was born in Manchester and lived there until I was sixteen, but I'd spent my adult life in New Zealand (where my parents had settled) and in Australia where I'd lived for the past thirteen years. I have to say life was treating me pretty well. Besides the business, I was in the middle of building my own house on fifty acres of land I'd bought in

Raymond Terrace, a town not far from Newcastle in the Australian Bush. I was very committed to environmental issues, and Miles and I cut timber for the house from the ironbark trees that grew on the land, using power we'd produced from the sun and wind and gas from a small sewage plant. So that even though the house was only half-finished and pretty primitive, all covered in building foil waiting to be clad, I felt content. I might have spent the past six months living in an incomplete house but at least I was following my dreams of an environmentally friendly future. Plus my home was in the middle of a forest full of koalas and exotic birds. How much more could you ask for?

Considering that this journey was to be the single most significant event of my life, I don't remember much about it. That's down to the injuries I received. All I recall is getting into the driver's seat of the van I drove to work and driving out of the car park. It was around 6pm. Miles was in the passenger seat and Stuart, a friend and part-time employee, was lying on a mattress in the back of the van. We were giving him a lift home. I remember there was some kind of banter going on between us, although I don't recall what it was about, and I said something cheeky to him as we drove out of the car park.

It was raining after a three-month-long dry spell. I know I drove the van along the industrial highway and slowed to stop at traffic lights where we were going to turn right on to an exit road. From then on I remember nothing at all.

Apparently, as we approached the junction, the lights changed to green. We entered the crossing, turning, but began to aquaplane over the wet road surface, even though we were only going at 43kph. We ended up slamming into a large industrial power pole just beyond the intersection. Stuart was propelled forwards by the impact into the back of my head, driving me into the steering wheel.

The steering wheel shattered, and spokes of wheel and indicator pierced my body in three places – through my throat up into the roof of my mouth, and through my right upper and lower thorax. My skull was crushed and I sustained multiple fractures.

Incredibly, Miles escaped with just a small seatbelt bruise. But Stuart's spine was broken in the accident, leaving him a quadriplegic. He remembers lying in the back of the van listening to Miles protecting him from being dragged out on to the road by the inevitable crowd of gawkers that had gathered after the accident. I'm very proud of Miles for that.

We were rushed to the hospital. My hospital admission notes make for gruesome reading: 'Massive compressed fracture Basal area, penetrating wound and fracture above and central to the eyebrows, severe damage to frontal lobes, olfactory bulbs destroyed, damage to thalamus. Right side zygoma [the area where the cheekbones meet the skull] has burst out of skull from apparent pressure, severe loss of brain matter from this wound. Right eye socket collapsed, right eye out of socket.'

I was placed on life support [a ventilator] in the emergency department and then transferred to the Intensive Care Unit where admittance tests were done.

At around 9.30pm they decided to test for brain death. Brain-death tests are done when they want to turn off machines, or use the living corpse for organ transplants. I understand they were hoping to use me for a donor.

Brain-death tests are not actually a pronouncement of death until the machines are turned off and breathing and heartbeat stop. They are complex tests that have to be done three or four times over several hours and they include fairly severe pain tests to find brain response to pain amongst other things.

My parents flew into Sydney from New Zealand at around 10am the next morning. As soon as the plane touched down, they rang the hospital and were asked for permission to donate my organs. When they refused, I was pronounced 'Dead'. Later, after they'd made the 200-mile journey from the airport to the hospital, they signed the official papers refusing transplant status.

My mother reports they met the professor of neurosurgery by appointment 'around lunchtime'. My father won't talk about what happened then. He's one of those men who turn white when they walk into a hospital. Even my mother, a midwife for forty years, doesn't like to talk about it. What happened there frightened her.

Apparently, they were shown into the professor's office, where he gave them the report of my death. He was trying to explain to them that they should be grateful as I would have been a 'vegetable' had I survived. During this very emotional conversation, a young, very agitated and frightened nurse came bursting into the office, blurting out, 'René is alive; she sat up and spoke!'

The professor was none too pleased about being interrupted and tried to shoo her away, lecturing her about how 'dead bodies' sometimes move and make noises. Three times he tried to resume talking to my parents, but the nurse was emphatic: 'René sat up and said, "Don't give me any more drugs!"' she reported.

At this point, my emotionally exhausted mother had had enough. She took the professor by his elbow, my father by his, and hurried them down the corridor to see what the nurse was talking about. They found me in a back corridor where I had apparently been placed so the nurse could remove equipment prior to my transfer to the morgue. I was by now in a deep coma, but I was breathing.

So how does such a thing happen in a large modern hospital? How does someone literally come back from the dead? We still don't have the answers. When my mum tried to get some sort of explanation from the doctors, the junior ones looked embarrassed and suggested someone made mistakes. The senior nurses confided that my notes had been changed.

The professor, meanwhile, seemed always to have an urgent appointment. My mother's attempts to talk to him resulted in a few muttered comments, but nothing that made sense. Perhaps that's understandable. You can't imagine a more embarrassing situation than breaking the news to parents that their child is dead, only to be told a moment later that the same child is sitting up and talking.

Mind you, his embarrassment was to get a lot worse. I remained in that initial coma for a further ten days before, to everyone's shock and amazement, I awoke once more. No one had expected me to regain consciousness for a second time. That's why no repairs had been carried out to my injuries – the chances of my surviving had still seemed so incredibly slim. It just didn't seem possible that I could have pulled through – but there I was.

I have some clear memories of what was going on around me during my time in the coma. I remember being aware of nurses and doctors around my bed talking about the possibility of me catching pneumonia and about how perhaps that would be the kindest thing.

I also remember the consultant on his morning rounds with

the junior doctors, talking about me as if I was a slab of meat on the bed. It was awful to hear. Worse was hearing my parents and Miles talking about me amongst themselves, and then talking to me as if I was a baby. I felt as if I was trapped down a big dark hole and was shouting at them to get me out, but no one could hear me.

When I actually awoke from the coma, sometime in the dead of night, I had a terrible need for the bathroom. My first conscious memories are of pulling a tube from my throat, hearing a machine making a breathing noise, tearing wires off my chest and finger, before hauling myself out of bed to find a bathroom.

Fortunately, the tubes which connected my arm to a drip were attached to a wheeled stand which followed me when I moved. I used it to help me manoeuvre myself up and wandered off in search of the bathroom, kicking a large plastic bag of fluid along the floor in front of me.

Eventually, I found a bathroom, and was frozen with horror at the open-skulled monster that confronted me in the mirror. I just couldn't comprehend that this could be me.

Then the nurse (who should have been watching me) arrived, screaming. 'What are you doing out of bed?' she yelled.

I was led back to the bed in a complete daze.

So where did I go during those lost days when I was considered 'dead' or else as good as dead? While my mangled body lay motionless on a hospital bed, barely able to function for itself, where was the essence that was me?

The truth was that I was somewhere else entirely, on a journey that took me way beyond the harsh lights and whirring machines of the hospital. I've no idea exactly when this journey began, or how long it lasted. All I know is that it was as real as anything that's ever happened to me, more real than life. While other memories have faded, this one is still more vivid to me than what happened yesterday.

I have no memory of the process of dying or leaving my body. All I know is I was moving head first through a dark maelstrom of what looked like black boiling clouds and feeling that I was being beckoned towards the darkness at the sides. I was quite frightened by this. I don't know what form I had, whether I had a body of any sort. Ahead was a tiny dot of bright light which steadily grew and brightened as I drew nearer. I became aware that I must be dead and was concerned for Mum and Dad and my sister. But I thought, 'They'll soon get over it.' It was a passing moment, just a fleeting thought as I rushed greedily forward towards this light.

I arrived in an explosion of glorious light into a room with insubstantial walls. The place was all white, but as if made of light, perhaps like standing inside a white eggshell illuminated from within and without. It's impossible to put my feelings into words but I was filled with this magnified sense of fascination and wonder, as if an exciting adventure was about to begin.

Standing before me was a man who looked to be in his thirties and about six feet tall. He had reddish-brown shoulder-length hair and an incredibly neat short beard and moustache. He wore a simple white robe and light seemed to emanate from him. I didn't know who he was, he didn't introduce himself or wear a name badge, but still it was like I knew him and he knew me.

I know that some people will try to make this image conform to their religious picture. All I can say is that I was, and am, Jewish but this wasn't a figure from any of the religious books or iconography I'd seen. According to my cultural expectations, I'd have been met by an old man with a big white beard, but this wasn't him.

Still, I felt this man had great age and wisdom and, when he stood before me, overpowering love, peace, contentment, welcome, empathy and joy radiated from him. I was awed and happy. I felt so very welcome, loved and even wanted. I felt I was home. These feelings and thoughts were overwhelming. There are no words I can find to describe the strength of the emotions going through me.

This man – I've since named him 'the gatekeeper' – welcomed me without words. I thought, 'I can sit at your feet forever and be content', which struck me even then as a strange thing to think/say/feel. I became fascinated by the fabric of his robe, trying to figure out how light could be woven like that.

He stood beside me and directed me to look to my left, where my life's less flattering moments were replayed to me. I relived all those moments and felt not only what I had done but also the hurt I had caused. I was surprised that some things I may have worried about weren't there, while casual remarks, which at the time I hadn't realised were hurtful, were counted.

For example, I painfully relived the hurt of a nursery teacher I'd spoken to unkindly. I relived my own actions, calling her a stupid fool for not listening to me, and then relived her sadness as she cried in private at home.

At the same nursery I turned over a large wooden rocking boat with children in it, because they wouldn't stop rocking to let me in. One of the children injured a wrist, and I relived both my own hurt feelings at not being allowed in and those of the children at being painfully thrown out.

In junior school, I reported a bully and exaggerated his

offence. That time my actions indirectly caused him to be hurt by his father. Again, I relived the feelings on both sides.

There are several other similar acts of spite over the years, as I pursued my own idea of justice. At around twenty-two, I swore at a policeman who was trying to book me for speeding. I got let off the ticket but apparently something in my vapid rant got too close to the truth, and he too was hurt by what I'd said.

And yet, surprisingly, some of the acts I remembered with most shame didn't appear in my life review. Once a school friend had persuaded me to steal a chocolate bar in order to become part of the group. I'd felt so guilty about it that I'd returned it to the shop, confessed to the shopkeeper and paid for it. At the time I'd felt incredibly worried and ashamed, and yet that wasn't mentioned in my life review.

While all these events were being played, I never felt judged. All I felt was my own guilt burdening me. Seeing this, the ever-loving gatekeeper directed me to look at kindnesses I had done, the acts of concern for others. I saw lives I'd saved or tried to save as a lifesaver and ambulance officer. I don't want to go into details of those, as I still feel bad for the times I didn't succeed. I chastise myself for learning new things too late.

Although I felt unworthy, it seemed the balance was in my favour and, throughout all these scenes from my life, good and bad, I received the same sense of great love.

After this, I was led further into the room, which became a hall, and there coming towards me was my grandfather. It was so wonderful to see my granddad. The harelip and cleft pallet that had marked his face when he was alive was gone and he looked younger than I'd ever known him and extremely joyful.

Though I wasn't aware of having a physical body, I felt his

hug and it made me rapturously happy. My granddad had died when I was fourteen and, until then, I hadn't realised how much anger I'd had at him for dying. He'd had heart problems and I'd promised him that I'd become a doctor when I grew up so that I could cure him. When he died, all that changed. I did my doctorates in philosophy, psychology, religion and culture, but never medicine. After we hugged, I felt moved to forgive him for dying and for making me break my promise to him.

Granddad told me that Grandma was coming soon and he was looking forward to her arrival. As far as I knew, Grandma was still in the best of health and doing her usual thing of spending summers in New Zealand and winters in Miami as she had done for a number of years. I couldn't understand why she'd be coming there.

So Granddad explained that she had cancer of the bowel and would be arriving shortly but he seemed to have no grasp of time and couldn't answer when I pressed for how soon. (In the event, Grandma was diagnosed three months later and died in August of that year.)

After Granddad and I had talked a while, he took me further into the room, which became a hall again, and we approached a group of people whom I vaguely recognised, although I don't know where from.

The person who'd been there to welcome me first, the gatekeeper, came and placed his hand on my shoulder and turned me towards him. Again I felt his touch, although I was still unaware of having a 'body'.

'You must return,' he told me. 'You have a task to perform.'

I was given no details of this task, no clue cards. I wanted to argue, I wanted to stay. I glanced back at Granddad but was propelled quickly towards the entrance. At the threshold, all became blackness. Then there was nothing, no awareness at all.

All this passed sometime during the course of that first coma. When I woke up I was still buoyed by my experiences. I don't remember much about the next three days but I know I talked ten-to-the-dozen about various things. I also know I blurted out the news about my grandma. I was still all excited about meeting Granddad and I told my mum that I'd met her father and that he was looking forward to seeing Grandma again after her impending death from bowel cancer. Don't forget that, at that time, the cancer was still undiagnosed so it wasn't a very kind or appropriate comment. But don't forget also that at this time I only had half a brain, and very little awareness of what I was saying or the effect it might have.

I think my mum was too overwhelmed by the fact that I'd regained consciousness at all to really take in what I'd said. Like the hospital staff, my parents couldn't really believe I'd come back from the coma. After two days of my being awake, they felt secure enough to go back to New Zealand where they had many things to sort out, having had to leave so suddenly. Then, on the third day, just hours after they'd flown back, I fell into a second coma caused by meningitis which had spread to my open wounds.

My poor parents received a phone call at home in New Zealand. 'There's no point in rushing back,' they were told. 'René won't last the next twenty-four hours.'

That second coma lasted another ten days. That was twenty-four years ago, and I'm still going.

The second coma was without any awareness at all. From my perspective I went to sleep one night and awoke the next morning, having lost ten days. I don't remember any of the details – not the fan which blew iced air over me constantly or the tent-like structure that covered the bed where I lay. It was Miles who would later fill me in on all of that. And there was no return to that 'other world', no gatekeeper welcoming me, or hugs from my grandfather. Just nothingness.

When I came round from that second coma, I was very angry. I was furious with G_d (that's how we write it in the Jewish religion) for sending me back. I felt as if I'd arrived 'home' when I was with Granddad. So why did he send me back so damaged and in so much pain?

Over the next few days and weeks I had three lots of surgery to repair my face, skull and eye socket. This was badly done and I've been left with Neanderthal eyebrows and lines on my forehead. I've since had operations to try to repair some of the damage. During plastic surgery in NZ a rib was used to build a new eye socket, and to fill in the gaps where the steering column had left a two-inch diameter hole in the skull above my eyes, but I'm still disfigured.

When I left hospital after just three months, I was still in intense pain and was suffering from double vision, anosmia (loss of the sense of smell) and damage to the eighth cranial nerve, which made me feel nauseous and affected my sense of balance.

I was discharged with no discharge plan, no information about how to rehabilitate myself, no information to help my partner Miles cope with the changes in his life. No effort was made to help me plan for and cope with these problems. Miles didn't understand at all.

I tried to go back to the business, but I couldn't cope with living, let alone working. Working for twenty minutes required two hours' sleep (on the floor). I did this all week and caught a bus home (fifty-two miles) on weekends, desperate to recover my business after so long away. It took me ages to discover that double vision isn't really conducive to success as an optical-instrument technician! It would probably have helped if someone had told me that before I started!

Some months after trying to restart work, I was told by the owner of the building where my workshop was situated that, as a death notice had been in the local paper, my premises had been re-let. I was given until the end of the month to move out. I then tried to open a new shop closer to home, but it was all just too difficult.

Miles had never really liked Australia. Now my accident made him have to accept responsibility for me. He was offered no assistance to help readjust to the massive changes in our lives. Nor was he prepared for such a major reversal of roles. I was disfigured, not really able to care for myself and no longer the nightclub raver I had once been. It wasn't long before I was on my own.

Miles returned to New Zealand to help with some family problems there. It must have been a relief for him to have some time to himself. To fill in my own time I would go 'shopping'. I was found in the street several times blankly staring into space. The real René wasn't there, just a zombie in her place.

I was still filled with anger at being sent back to all this suffering, and still trying to come to terms with seeing double – twins instead of individuals, two roads instead of one. Three months after leaving hospital I tried to end it all, hoping I'd get back to the state of bliss I'd found during my NDE. I took a shotgun and pulled the trigger, but, instead of the bang I was expecting, there was just a click. I cursed G_d at denying me even this relief.

My life was out of control. No one knew how to help me. Eventually, some nuns I met suggested that I have myself 'committed' to a psychiatric clinic where I could be cared for. I hadn't been there long when my mother, alarmed at the way I'd disappeared from her radar, came to Australia to find me. Seeing the state I was in, she collected me and took me back to Auckland, New Zealand. That was in December 1982.

I suppose Mum felt that I needed to be cared for. She was right. I had been living as if in a pit. The things I had suffered should not have occurred, *need* not have occurred. It wasn't that the care system didn't work; it just wasn't there in the first place. Mum provided care, total cotton wool, a safety net. For a short time I luxuriated in the security she provided. I needed it after feeling so completely alone.

Dad didn't cope well with the accident, or with the fact his pride and joy had now returned home at the age of thirty-five, as a child again. We had always crossed intellectual swords, but after my brain injury I was too withdrawn and Dad was too disappointed for the relationship to flourish; I felt he avoided me.

I was like a kind of zombie. I spent my time staring into space without seeing anything, drooling to myself until my attention was grabbed when I was spoken to when I'd rouse myself to respond. Then it would take me ages to work out who and where I was so I'd have to ask people to repeat what they'd asked of me. Then, because I only had a ten-second attention span, I'd lose concentration again between the question and the answer.

It was hard for Mum and Dad. They made the mistake of doing everything for me so that I ended up with willing slaves who allowed me to opt out of life. They didn't realise — and neither did I at that stage – that the effort involved in struggling to make my battered brain function was essential for my development. You must force the brain to find another way to route the tasks that need to be done. There is no other way to relearn the basics of living.

I grew more and more angry at my circumstances. I despised myself for how I found myself. I was angry at G_d and upset by my parents making themselves my slaves and looking after me too well – which denied me the opportunity to take responsibility for myself. But of course I couldn't express any of it.

So, when Miles, who was now living in Hamilton, New Zealand, asked me to move in with him once again two months later, I jumped at the chance of regaining some independence.

Relearning was a struggle but also an adventure. The first cup of coffee I made alone took me four hours. I kept losing concentration between putting the kettle on and getting a mug. I'd keep up a running commentary to myself: 'I am making coffee, jug is on, need a mug.' Then I'd look at the cupboard, forget what I needed, panic and have to start again: 'I am making coffee. I need a mug.' I repeated this procedure countless times hovering between the two-pronged axis of the mug cupboard and the coffee jug. Then I had to start it all again when it was time to go and look for a spoon. Eventually, hours later, the coffee was made. It was then I discovered that Miles had been watching me patiently all that time. It must have taken a heroic effort not to step in and help me when he saw me struggling again and again to perform such tiny tasks, but he'd made himself step back.

'Well done,' he told me proudly. Then he made us both a sandwich and himself a coffee and we sat and ate and drank.

And so it went for years with me pushing myself forward in

a series of tiny victories and Miles being supportive in his hands-off way, helping only if I asked.

The turning point came in 1984 when I was watching Fred Flintstone on television. It annoyed me that I was unable to follow the story of this simple cartoon. I got angry with myself. I had those university degrees yet couldn't keep up with a children's cartoon. I threw all my tablets – for pain, for balance, for depression – down the toilet. I was going to try a new way. The next day I bought a computer and some educational programs for teenagers. I sat at that computer every day, for hours, stringing together thoughts and actions to master the simple programs. I bought a diary program and used it to organise my life, reminding me of everything I had to do each moment. That computer and subsequent computers have become my subsidiary brain. I still carry a Psion pocket book.

Miles was there throughout my recovery but, inevitably, our relationship started to dissolve. I'd lost my libido and Miles had to put up with a partner who constantly made excuses to avoid physical contact, who always told him, 'Wait till I finish this chapter.'

I could no longer stand noisy crowded places. I would become confused and need to go home. I could no longer dance as my balance centres were shot and I hadn't yet learned how to compensate to redress the balance. So for several years he went out while I preferred to stay home. No wonder we drifted apart. Eventually, Miles became more and more distant and no longer initiated any close contact. With hindsight, it's surprising our relationship lasted so long. Miles left for greener pastures in November 1995. We had been together for eighteen years. Not bad I think, considering all the problems we had. I still miss his friendship and company.

In 1986 I managed to find work experience at a large hospital in New Zealand as a service technician in the anaesthetic department. This led to full-time work in January 1987. I moved to the adult ICU to work as a technician later that year and to the Newborn ICU in 1989, looking after the life-support equipment. It was good to be active again, and I even managed to come up with some modifications that greatly improved the effectiveness of the equipment. However, relations with other staff members were sometimes difficult. The frontal-lobe damage I'd sustained can make me seem abrupt and blunt, and occasionally people take offence where none is meant.

In 2000 an incident led to me being suspended and I was dismissed in June 2001.

However, I kept busy. Spurred on by the lack of support available to me when I left hospital, I've also been instrumental in setting up the Head Injury Society of New Zealand so that hopefully no one else will have to go through the loneliness and isolation that I and my family faced all those years ago. And I've been involved with causes I believe in, like getting the cycle helmet laws changed and the disability act.

And yet, I don't believe any of this is my 'task'. Sadly, I'm no nearer discovering what that task is. All I can think is that it is to live with new awareness, giving kindness where I can.

I still haven't completely come to terms with what happened to me, or the fact I've been left permanently disfigured by the accident, the operations and the fact that having my face stripped from my skull three times during reconstructive surgery has left the skin wrinkled. I guess age hasn't helped either.

If I had the funds I might consider some cosmetic surgery, but

I'm more resigned now than I used to be. There's no point stressing over things we can't change.

I think still about where I went during my NDE. I used to try to make 'deals' with G_d to get back there. I'd say, 'If I do this to help other people, or get involved with this cause, can I then come "home"?'

But it doesn't work. Obviously the key to my 'task' doesn't lie in politics or working for disabled people. Perhaps after all it is just being kind to others and helping where I can.

I've always been intuitive. When I was a child, my mother was scared by my ability to foretell things that hadn't happened, as she wrote in her diary. The near-death experience took away whatever barrier or fear about this intuitiveness had been instilled by my childhood. I now 'see' or sense the same things as when I was little, but with an adult awareness. I am able to see when people need a kind word, or reassurance or a soothing touch. But I don't want people to seek me out for any kind of 'healing'. In the end, all results come from within those people themselves – from their own belief, trust or faith.

My experience has changed how I view religion. I don't believe there's one 'right' religion. I think that, if people have a religion they believe in, then it's important for them to live by those beliefs and not just pay lip service to them. And, if they can't live by their beliefs, they should find a moral structure they *can* live by.

And, of course, I have no more fear of death, apart from perhaps some concern that it shouldn't be too slow.

I just pray that, whatever my 'task' may be, it's completed soon so that I can be released from the struggle that is my life.

I want to return home.

# 6

# JO CLEMENSON, 43
## PSYCHOLOGIST, SPAIN

I'VE GOT A letter somewhere — at least I think I still have it; I don't remember throwing it away. It's from London Transport and it kindly informs me that the company will not be taking legal action against me for damaging one of their double-decker buses. Which was very big of them considering I'd apparently made a big dent and a few nasty scratches on the front of the bus — with the side of my head!

Yep, I was knocked over by a double-decker bus. Sounds like a comedy, doesn't it? But at the time it wasn't funny.

It was back in 1989, February or March, and I was twenty-seven years old. I was working for a finance company in Wimpole Street, central London — in my book, just having a job in finance is enough to mean I deserved to get run over by a great big bus! As you can probably tell, I hated work, but it was a way to make money.

I'd been for a drink with some friends from work in a basement bar round the corner from the office. I'd wanted to get home early, so I'd only stayed for one drink before getting off. I was heading in the direction of Oxford Street tube station, but I was keeping an eye out in case a bus came along that was going my way – to Kennington.

I walked along a side street towards Oxford Street – it was one of the side streets that a lot of buses come along before getting to the main road. I remember there was a pub at the corner and, as I got to it, I looked behind and saw my bus approaching, so I started to cross the road and that's the last thing I remember.

I was reading something interesting the other day about how very few people who get knocked down actually remember the minutes beforehand and the twenty minutes afterwards. It's something to do with the brain shutting off to protect you, which means most people don't have any memory of actually being hit.

According to the bus driver, I just walked out in front of the bus, but I don't remember anything about it at all. One minute I was looking across the road, ready to cross and then that's it until I woke up in hospital.

Apparently, the front of the bus hit me on the left side of my head and I was tossed into the air. I ended up lying in the road, unconscious.

The next thing I knew I was waking up in University College Hospital. I knew it must have been some time later because my mum was there – calm as ever, but obviously tremendously relieved to see me awake.

'I've seen Grandma!' I told her excitedly. And it was true.

While I was unconscious, I'd met with my grandmother

who'd died about five years before. The two of us had had our ups and downs while she was still alive, but we'd stayed pretty close. So I suppose it wasn't surprising that, when the bus hit me, it was my grandmother who came to meet me. But I don't remember the actual moment when we were reunited – I just remember being with her. We were in what I can only describe as a sort of park. It was a beautiful day, absolutely lovely.

My grandma looked very similar to how I'd seen her before, perhaps a little bit younger. I don't remember exactly what she was wearing but her clothes were familiar, things I'd seen her in before. We were standing up, talking, just like I'd talk to anyone 'real' and physical.

It was very beautiful where I was. I know that wherever I was it was somewhere I wanted to stay. I was completely drawn to where I was. I didn't have any inkling that I wanted to get back. I felt really at peace. I felt it was where I belonged. It was a sense of coming home. It was almost like a meditative state. There was a real sense of knowing who you were, as if you'd taken away the outer cover and revealed the real person. I felt at ease, totally comfortable.

There was no fear, no worry about the unknown. I was happy to see her. I didn't wonder where I was at all. At one level, I recognised completely who I was and where I was. It was a really familiar feeling, not at all alarming.

We talked about things that I can't remember now. As soon as I woke up, I told my mum many, many things because it was all very vivid in my mind. I told her how her mum was and all the things she'd told me. But now I don't recall all the details. The one thing I do remember very, very clearly to this day is her saying to me, 'It isn't your time yet. You still have a lot of work to do and you have to go back.'

I completely understood it. It was a slight sense of loss that I had to leave this place, but on the other hand I knew in myself that, yes, it was exactly right, that it wasn't my time. I didn't feel cheated or anything. I accepted that I still had a lot of experiences to go through.

She came across as being very wise and calm. She was like that in real life but not to the same extent. Again, she was recognisable as my grandmother, very much so, but it just felt like there was a lot more wisdom and gentleness there than had been the case in real life.

Soon after, I suddenly woke up. There's no transitional memory of going back into my body or anything.

When I woke up, I had no idea where I was. Initially, I thought I was at the dentist because there were lots of people in white coats standing around and my teeth really ached, but I guess that was just the impact of the bus. There were also a couple of policemen there who wanted to know if I'd been drinking. I still think that's a bit much that they couldn't have waited until the next day.

Then I saw my mum and told her excitedly all about seeing my grandmother. I had a very long conversation with her apparently, filling her in on all the things we'd talked about, although I don't remember them now. Luckily, my mum had her own very strong belief in the afterlife so to her it was something that was completely normal. It didn't freak her out at all. And, as a former nurse, she wasn't upset by the hospital environment.

Later I found out that someone from work had left the bar soon after me, saw what happened and went running back to tell my friend who then rang my mum. My friend, bless him, called my mum and told her I'd been hit by a car – he'd been a hospital porter in the past and knew the damage a bus could do, and he hadn't wanted to panic her too much by mentioning the word 'bus'.

I had surprisingly few injuries considering I'd been hit on the side of my head by a bus and thrown through the air. I had severe whiplash and one or two very deep cuts. I also had massive bruising – oddly, this wasn't on the side of my face that had been hit by the bus, but on my right side where I'd landed on the road. In fact, my face swelled up like the elephant man for a few days after my accident. I remember the nurse telling me not to look in the mirror when I dragged myself to the bathroom. As if you're not going to look when someone tells you that. I was horrified at the deformed creature that looked back at me – but at least I knew that it was just swollen and would eventually go back to normal.

The doctors kept me in hospital for a week doing repeated scans. They were so convinced that you couldn't get hit on the side of the head by a double-decker bus and not suffer damage to the skull or the brain, but I was just lucky, I guess.

Apparently, the bus driver locked himself in the bus straight after knocking me down because a group of guys in the pub had tried to beat him up. They'd claimed the bus came swerving round the corner, but, of course, I have no way of knowing if that was right because I just can't remember. Then a few weeks later I got that letter from London Transport saying they wouldn't be suing me for damage to the bus. You have to laugh.

The experience felt very different to a dream. It really did feel like you were physically there rather than watching yourself there, which is often the case in a dream where you're dreaming it, but you're also the watcher. It felt completely normal.

Perhaps the sounds and colours were slightly enhanced, but it was real.

I do believe that a part of me – a soul or a spirit – left my body when the bus hit me and I do believe my grandmother was there. But I think our brain interprets things in a certain way that we see this as reality when it's not necessarily reality. I don't think it's the case that we go somewhere else after we die – heaven or wherever. I believe there are other dimensions here right now all around us operating on different frequencies. It's only through other experiences – drugs or schizophrenia or, like in my case, nearly dying – that we become able to see these other dimensions, even if it's just temporary.

I wouldn't be surprised if there were also other time dimensions. I remember my friend's parents, who were quite straight-laced, telling me about this holiday they'd had in Devon or Cornwall. They'd found this little shop that sold shells and fossils and the whole family had walked into it and had a look around. They spoke to the old man who worked there. Then they left and the next day they decided to go back to it. The shop wasn't there. They were convinced it was the right corner but instead there was a newsagents there. They couldn't understand it. They went to the local pub and spoke to the man behind the bar. The place they were describing, that shop, had been on that corner thirty years ago. They described the man and everything fitted in with the description. I believe that kind of time lapse can happen.

The experience I had hasn't really affected my life but that's only because I was brought up in the type of family that was quite open to all these things. My grandmother was Jewish, but became a Buddhist, so we always had respect for many different religions and talked a lot about spiritual and esoteric things. I can imagine, if I hadn't had that kind of upbringing, my experience would have been really life-changing because it confirms that life does go on.

I don't worry myself about what the 'work' is that I have to do. At the time, I remember feeling like there must be a specific thing I was sent back for, that it wasn't just experiences, but I don't think that now. I think it's about achieving your full potential. I've had two children since then, and that could be part of the experience I've been sent back to have, but I don't think that was my sole purpose or anything.

I think it's interesting that my grandmother used the phrase 'it's not your time yet'. Now I've read quite a bit about NDE I know that particular phrase features quite a lot, but, in the late 1980s, there wasn't much interest in NDE and I'd never heard about it. If I'd known about it before, I might be able to accept that I already had it in my mind before I was hit by the bus, but, at that stage, I had absolutely no knowledge of it. All the scientific theories about brain chemistry and lack of oxygen can't explain the fact that I knew nothing about NDE and yet my grandmother clearly told me the same phrase that so many other people have reported hearing during their own NDEs.

I've never really had a fear of dying, so I can't say my NDE made any difference to that. I believe we just take off our physical shells and shift dimensions. When my mum had a brain haemorrhage a few years ago, she was left completely paralysed. Yet, about ten minutes before she died, she sat up and smiled this most blissful smile. Then she lay back and gently closed her eyes. There's nothing to be scared of.

# 7

## PAT LOVEDAY, 61
### PSYCHIATRIC NURSE, READING

I'VE ALWAYS HAD a tremendous fear of death. My own mother died when she was around my age and my greatest worry was that the same thing would happen to me – that I'd be prematurely taken away from my four children and grandchildren.

Now it makes me shiver to think how close I came to that deep-seated fear coming true. And yet, thanks to coincidence, or fate, or whatever you might choose to call it, I'm still here. All I can think is that maybe everybody has a time – and this just wasn't mine.

My nightmare began on Tuesday, 7 September 2005 when I was booked into hospital in Berkshire for a minor operation to straighten my foot following bunion surgery the year before. The operation was all carried out under local anaesthetic and seemed to have gone without a hitch. I was told I'd be in plaster for six weeks afterwards and would need crutches to get around. I was also given a supply of strong painkillers to get me through the next few days.

At first, everything happened just as they'd said. I had no pain, thanks to the painkillers, and was pleased that the surgery was over and done with and I could look forward to getting back to normal. But on the Thursday I started to feel some pain in my foot and by Thursday evening it had become excruciating. It really felt like there was somebody sawing my foot.

After a disturbed night sleeping on the sofa, I rang the surgeon who'd carried out the operation to tell him I couldn't cope with the pain.

'You shouldn't be experiencing that degree of pain,' he told me, and he prescribed stronger painkillers which a friend picked up for me.

But, even with the new painkillers, the pain was unbearable. On the Friday night, my younger daughter was supposed to be staying with me but she was out and didn't have a key to get back in. I hauled myself up to bed but sometime in the night I woke up. The combination of strong painkillers and intense pain I was experiencing at that time makes it difficult to piece together the exact chronology of what happened. I remember falling over as I tried to get out of bed. Then I remember going to the bathroom for a drink and being on the floor of the bathroom. At some point, I went downstairs sitting down, and I dragged myself to the sofa where I lay semi-comatose, unable to think or act.

Though I didn't know it at this stage, my body was slowly being consumed by a flesh-eating virus called necrotising fasciitis, a severe and extremely aggressive streptococcal infection which starts in a wound or broken skin. If I'd lain on that sofa much longer, the doctors later told me, I'd certainly be dead now.

As it was, at lunchtime, my older daughter Mandy arrived. Although she hadn't been due to come round until that evening, something had prompted her to change her mind. To this day, she has no idea what it was – she never normally makes unscheduled visits – but she just felt she had to see me. Thank goodness she did.

As soon as Mandy came through the door, she knew something was very wrong indeed.

'Who am I?' she asked me urgently, trying to assess just how out of it I was.

'Mandy,' I replied.

'And what's your grandson's name?' she queried.

'Jim,' I told her. His name is actually Kieran. Mandy knew then that I needed help quickly, and called an ambulance. That's the last thing I remember.

Back at the hospital, staff opened up the plaster around my foot. The stitches had totally disappeared and the wound was now gaping open. They needed to get me straight into ITU but there were no beds available, so I was transferred to a hospital in Oxford.

I must have passed out but then I remember coming round to find a doctor asking me whether my foot had looked the same the last time I'd seen it. I glanced down.

'No,' I told him. 'It was completely different then. It wasn't black.'

That's my last conscious memory. A friend who came to visit the next day tells me that I appeared to be okay and perfectly lucid and that, when the doctor told me I had gangrene and needed immediate surgery and might lose my foot, I readily consented. I remember none of that.

By the Sunday afternoon, I'd lost my foot but there was still a danger that they hadn't caught the infection, so they kept a constant watch on the wound. Within an hour, another two inches of my leg had turned black. I was taken back to surgery and lost half of my leg. This time there was no further spread of the infection and, after almost twenty-four hours, my wound was sewn up.

But that didn't mean I was out of danger. Within hours, my vital organs had failed. My kidneys and lungs had packed up and I was attached to a ventilator. My sister and brother and children were called in and kept a constant rolling vigil. I wasn't expected to survive.

For the next twelve days I hung there in that state – neither dead, nor really living. The medical staff were constantly monitoring me. Yet, though they were acutely aware of the trauma that my physical body was experiencing, they could have no idea that, inside my mind, my psyche was going through an altogether more terrifying ordeal.

With the benefit of hindsight and my experience as a psychiatric nurse I know that this living hell I endured for twelve long days and nights was most likely a product of drug-induced psychosis. After all, I was on very high levels of potent medication. However, drug-related or not, there are moments of it when I am utterly convinced I came face to face with death and was given a clear and conscious choice whether to give in to it, or to fight on for life. Those were the moments when the staff called my family to my hospital bed to say their goodbyes. If I didn't actually die, I'd come as near as you can get and still survive.

And yet there were times during those days when I was sure I wouldn't pull through and when I begged for it all to end. It was, without exaggeration, the most horrendous experience of my life.

It started with my being convinced I was in the South of France with my daughter and her partner. In 'real' life we'd recently visited Florida, but when I recovered consciousness I remained completely sure it was actually the South of France we'd been to. It was all that real.

While in the South of France, I became unwell and was taken to a private clinic where I was told I could be treated, but I'd need to give them £27,000. Later, this too seemed real and I bombarded my daughter with questions about how she'd raised the money.

While in the clinic, I was attached to a monitor for testing, but was horrified when messages began to appear telling me that I had three questions to answer and, depending on how well I answered them, three members of my family would either be saved or killed.

I was utterly terrified. I know it sounds mad, but it was so real I honestly thought my family's lives were in my hands.

After that I was in a nursery, tied to a bed, being shown pictures of children who were supposed to be my grandchildren – but they weren't anything like them. When I said, 'No, that's not them', the pictures would be changed slightly to see if it made any difference.

Then I was in a dining room. The only person who came to see me there was my friend Elaine. We were allowed to go out sometimes for a cigarette. But then it got to the stage where she was allowed out, but I wasn't. I could see her outside and I remember crying, 'Get me out. Please get me out.' I felt totally abandoned.

The whole experience lasted days and days and the terror never ever let up. I never saw who 'they' were – the ones who were trying to kill me and my family, but I knew they were evil and that they were capable of doing everything they threatened.

I was tested constantly. Like I'd get a message through the

monitor at the clinic saying, 'We'll only do such and such if you agree to the Pope dying.' The tests always involved someone being killed. And it was always my responsibility.

I used to beg 'them', whoever they were, to kill me because I just couldn't stand it any more.

But it was the threats to my family that were the worst. Apparently, in my semi-conscious state lying on the hospital bed, I'd yell out to my daughters or sons to keep away from me. I'd be very rude and use foul language, which must have been really upsetting for them, but to me it was the only way to keep them safe. At times 'they' would tell me to nominate members of my family to be killed – if I didn't choose, they'd all die anyway.

At one stage in my nightmare world, my eldest daughter opened a door at the end of the ward, and dropped straight through into the open air, committing suicide. When two friends came to see me, I asked them to open the door and look outside.

'We can see Mandy,' they told me. 'She's lying there, covered in blood.'

It was constant psychological torture in which reality would get mixed up with unreality and life with death. One time my brother was sitting with me in the 'real' world and talking about our mother who'd died when she was about my age.

'She and Dad wouldn't want you to join them yet,' he urged me. 'It's not time. It's too soon.'

But in my mind it was the man in the bed opposite who was talking about my mother.

'Shut up,' I yelled at him. 'Keep quiet.'

In the end, it came to the point when I couldn't go on any longer. I was at rock bottom, completely exhausted by the never-ending mind-games I'd been put through. This is the point at which, I'm convinced, the medical staff warned my family I probably wouldn't make it.

I knew that I was facing a stark choice – to live, even though I believed that my family had all been killed, or to die and join them. I chose to live.

'You're not going to kill me,' I told them.

In my mind, even if I didn't have any family left, I knew I had to come back to look after my dog, Polly.

That's how it was that my first lucid comment on coming back to the 'real' world was to ask after Polly. It's a standing joke with my kids now that, despite having four children and four grandchildren, ultimately it was the dog who came first.

My first clear memory of waking up was a nurse asking me if my son could come in and see me. During my 'dream' time, I'd often shouted at my family to clear off, trying to keep them away from me and out of danger.

This time I said 'yes' and, when he came in, I cried and cried because I'd been convinced I didn't have any family left.

When I woke up, twelve days after I'd gone into hospital, I had no idea that my foot had been amputated. In fact, it's funny, I could still feel it. The stump of my leg was heavily bandaged and there were sheets covering me up, but my foot felt like it was still there. It was a doctor who broke the news to me.

'You've been extremely ill,' he told me. 'We've had to remove your foot.'

It's a sign of just how relieved I was to be out of the nightmare of my dream state that I wasn't unduly upset by this news. I remember thinking, 'That's okay. At least I'm still alive.' Even now, a few months on, when the reality of living with a disability is starting to sink in, I still believe the hardest part of my experience was the dreaming, not the actual physical amputation or its consequences.

My tormentors had repeatedly told me that if I told anyone what was happening they'd all be killed, so it was a couple of days before I dared mention my ordeal. That's how powerful a hold it had over me – even fully conscious and surrounded by family, I still believed it had been real.

I can't describe the relief when I finally realised it had all been in my head. It had been so terrifying. But still I fought against going to sleep, for fear of finding myself back in the nightmare.

'It's okay, we'll stay with you while you sleep,' my youngest daughter told me, but it wasn't enough to conquer the terror I felt at the idea of finding myself once again in what I called 'my bit of hell'. In the end, the doctors had to prescribe sleeping medication to knock me out – I still take that now. I don't want to take the risk of dreaming.

I remained in hospital a further five weeks – first in Oxford, then back in Reading. When I came out, my youngest daughter came to stay with me to help me adjust. I'm gradually coming to terms with the physical consequences of what happened to me, but the mental scars are nowhere near healed. Unlike a dream, the memories of my experience haven't faded at all. It still feels just as real as ever.

Like I said before, I was always terrified of dying prematurely – like my mum before me. My experience in hospital has made that fear a million times worse.

I'm a psychiatric nurse myself so I know what I experienced was largely a drug-induced psychosis. But I also think that, because I came so close to death – practically one foot in the door – it was something more. I didn't see any shining lights or tunnels, but I saw death close up – and I chose life.

# 8

# GEORGINA DIXON, 48
## HOMEOPATH, BRISTOL

THERE'S A BOOK CALLED *Families and How to Survive Them*. That's the book I ought to have written. Or maybe I could get one of those T-shirts made up – 'I survived my family'. That would be good. Mind you, I suppose everyone has skeletons in their closets.

I was the eldest of four children, the youngest two of whom were adopted. My parents cared for all of us just the same, but my youngest brother, Nathan, developed a real chip on his shoulder. He felt everyone was against him, everyone had it in for him. 'What would *you* know about it?' was his favourite line, as if he'd cornered the market in hardship.

Being the eldest, I'd already left home when things really started to go wrong for Nathan. Always an 'all or nothing' person, he developed a problem with alcohol and drugs. Off them, he was sensitive and loving but, when he was using, he changed completely, becoming confrontational and aggressive.

In Nathan's world, nobody understood him, nobody knew what he was going through. If my parents refused to give him money for drink or drugs, it was because they hated him, or because he'd never been good enough for them, or because they always gave stuff to everyone else except him.

In time, Nathan was diagnosed with a personality disorder and was put on medication. For a while, this calmed him down, but the problems with drink and drugs never really went away. When he'd been drinking, he'd get into fights with everyone around him, alienating most of his friends and getting him into endless trouble with the police.

It would be nice to say that my own life, by contrast, was a model of domestic bliss, but that would be being rather too economical with the truth! True, I set up a thriving practice as a homeopath, but, on the home front, things were far from harmonious. I'd got married and had two gorgeous children, but after thirteen years my relationship with my husband had started to fall apart, and by 2003 we were in the middle of an incredibly vicious and destructive divorce. The children, by this time aged twelve and fourteen, were caught in the centre of a bitter tug-of-war, which sadly ended up in the law courts not once, but seven harrowing times. I guess we both tried to protect them but, when feelings run so deep, it becomes next to impossible.

So, you could say I was feeling pretty low and emotionally drained when, in May 2003, I decided to take the kids to my parents' for a weekend. I thought it would be a chance for me to relax and recuperate, away from the stresses of home. How wrong can you be?

When I arrived at my parents' house, it was far from the haven of peace and tranquillity I'd been craving. Nathan, facing a charge of assaulting a friend, was back living at home as part of his bail conditions. By this stage, he'd already served time in prison and my parents were desperate to keep him from going in again. But, as the date of the next hearing drew nearer, he became more and more agitated, convinced he was heading back to prison.

Walking through the front door with my bags, I immediately felt the tension in the atmosphere as if it were a solid force, pushing down on me. My heart sank.

Over the course of the weekend, things got steadily worse. I didn't know it then but his psychologist had changed his medication and Nathan hadn't taken any of his anger-management drugs for thirty-six hours. Not surprisingly, he was completely on edge – the tiniest comments could set him off on a huge rant. His girlfriend, Chrissie, who was staying with him at my mum and dad's, couldn't do anything to calm him down. Like the rest of us, she tiptoed around him as if walking on fragile ice that could crack at any moment.

My children, fortunately, had always idolised Nathan, seeing him as a kind of 'rebel without a cause' figure, so they weren't scared of what was going on, although of course they sensed the tension in the air. But, for the rest of us, it was a really difficult couple of days.

On the Sunday, Nathan was acting in a particularly surly manner, doing little niggly things to try to wind us all up.

I remember him walking up the stairs in front of me and deliberately standing there playing with his phone so I couldn't get past. I knew there was no point in saying anything; I just waited for him to make his point and continue on up the stairs.

Later on, I was downstairs writing up some outstanding

homeopathy case notes when Nathan came into the living room. Immediately he launched into his favourite subject – how I didn't understand any of his problems, how the world and his wife were against him. On and on. I'd heard it all so many times before. It was his way of justifying his actions to himself, so he could disown his violence, claiming that circumstances had made him do it. Well, I had problems enough of my own.

'Just go away,' I told him, and carried on writing my notes.

Of course, that just set Nathan off into a self-pitying, increasingly angry tirade. My dad came in to try to defuse the situation – something he was an old hand at. But Nathan wasn't having any of it. Really worked up now, he grabbed my dad and pushed him out into the hall, holding the door shut behind him so I couldn't get out to see what was going on.

From the other side of the door, I heard my father cry out in pain. Bursting into the hall, I found Dad on the floor clutching his right shoulder. My brother, by this point, was standing a few feet away, trying to look as if nothing had happened.

'Are you okay?' I asked my father, bending down to check.

'Yes, I think so,' came the stunned reply.

Whirling round, I faced Nathan. 'What the hell do you think you're playing at?' I snarled at him. And that's when it all started, that's when Nathan attacked me.

Later I was diagnosed as having suffered concussion during the attack, so the details of what happened are still hazy but I have an overriding memory of how terrifying it was. I guess all attacks are brutal and horrific, but, when violence has never been part of your life and when it comes out of the blue without a chance to prepare for it, it's extremely traumatic.

I didn't see Nathan coming for me. I was probably bending back down again to help my father up. That would have been my natural inclination anyway. I have a vague recollection of being carried over to the other side of the hall and slammed against the wall – again and again and again.

At some point I lost consciousness. The next recollection I have is coming to with my brother still hammering me into the wall, my hands flopped down by my side. I was like a marionette, floppy and completely bewildered. I remember staring at my brother in the throes of the attack thinking, 'What is going on?' as I was rammed into the wall over and over again. I looked into his eyes, searching for some glimmer of recognition that I was his sister, that I didn't deserve this, but there was nothing, no hint of emotion – almost as if he had been taken over by a malevolent entity.

While my brother was attacking me it was chaos all around with my father and Chrissie both trying to restrain him.

'Stop it, stop it,' they were shouting, but he's a big strong man with a history of violence, so even the two of them together didn't have much effect. It was only when my daughter came out of the lounge to see what all the noise was about that he finally came to his senses and stopped. After flinging me on to the floor, he stormed off.

It was while I was lying there, drifting in and out of consciousness, that I had this bizarre experience. Suddenly I was outside of my body, somewhere up near the ceiling. I wasn't aware of having a body at all when I was looking down from above. It was as if my mind was separated from my body – the thinking, conscious being that was 'me' looking down on the physical aspect of my body.

As I gazed down on myself lying in a heap on the floor, I knew it was me, but at the same time I knew there was something different about me. It wasn't until later, when I tried to make sense of what happened, that I realised exactly what the difference was. My hair, which was dyed blonde at this time, had reverted to its natural colour. The 'me' I was looking down on was a brunette.

Also, at the same time as I saw myself slumped on the floor, I saw myself holding out my right hand out as if to say, 'Please help me.'

To this day, I don't know whether I was holding my hand out to the others around me or to this other spiritual 'self' – what I now believe was my life force, hovering up near the ceiling, trying to rejoin it to my body.

Then, all of a sudden, I was back in my body. I don't remember any noise or any sensation that signified a 're-entry', just one minute I was looking down on myself and the next I was lying on the floor gazing up. I knew immediately that I was hurt. All my insides felt like they'd been beaten around and put back in the wrong place. But my anger was stronger than any physical discomfort. I remember putting my right hand behind my body and levering myself up to my feet. By now, my family was huddled around Nathan trying to stop him from renewing his attack. I hobbled over to my mobile which was on charge in the hall, dialled 999 and asked the operator for the police.

Brandishing the phone at Nathan, I shouted, 'I've called the police.'

But, before the operator could put me through, my dad wrestled the phone from me and cut the call off. 'We can't involve the police, he's already in enough trouble. They'll send him straight back to prison.'

I couldn't believe it. My body was aching all over, my head throbbed. I'd been brutally, viciously attacked and yet my brother was going to get off scot-free.

I insisted on driving home even though I was still in shock. My instinct was to get the kids out of my parents' house as soon as I possibly could. But, once I was home, my symptoms became progressively worse. I remember lying in bed that evening with severe pains shooting up and down my arms and legs. I was terrified to go to sleep in case I woke up and couldn't move.

I'd never felt so vulnerable. I knew I needed to go to hospital, but, as a single parent, I didn't want to leave the kids in the night or drag them to casualty with me. They'd been through enough witnessing the assault. In the end, I phoned some elderly friends in the early hours of the morning, and one of them came over to be with the kids while I went to casualty where they X-rayed my back and neck.

The X-rays showed nothing was broken, and yet I was racked with pain. The following day I managed to get an appointment with an osteopath. He was shocked at the way my skeletal frame had been left misaligned after the attack.

'You're lucky not to have broken your neck,' he told me.

My spine had been damaged in the attack, and this affected my lower back. My body was racked with constant pain on the left side, with pains extending down my left leg. For the next few months, the only way I could work was by standing on one leg, like a stork.

Before the attack, I'd been super-fit, working out three or

four times a week. After it, I was virtually crippled – even sitting down caused severe discomfort. It would be six long months before I recovered even a fraction of my former mobility.

But worse than the physical pain were the emotional scars. I went over and over the attack in my head, reliving the fear and the feeling of powerlessness and the anger. At nights, I'd wake up with the image of myself lying on the floor of the hall, my hair dull brown, my hand held out in a plea for help.

Although I refused to go back to my parents' house, I was in contact with them and knew that my brother was becoming increasingly unpredictable. His relationship with Chrissie, who was still living with my parents, was more and more volatile and I worried constantly about my parents' safety. My mother was frail and disabled and my brother was a strong violent man with addiction problems. What if he attacked them and no one was there to defend them?

After a lot of soul searching, I made the difficult decision to report the attack to the police. I knew, even as I was making my statement, that I could be jeopardising my relationship with my parents but I couldn't bear to think of them being in danger, or even of him attacking some stranger in the street.

The policeman was very kind, but I felt sick as I gave my brother's name and address. I knew my parents would find it really hard to accept.

Sure enough, my dad stopped talking to me after my brother was arrested for the attack. He'd spent the last twenty years of his life trying to protect his adopted son and he was furious I'd done something which would add to Nathan's criminal record.

But I knew this was something I had to do. I was even prepared to go to court to testify against him, but in the end it wasn't necessary. By this stage, Nathan had committed so many crimes, the attack on me was just a kind of footnote.

Nathan was sentenced to four years imprisonment. My father was completely devastated and refused to have any contact with me. My mother would send me short letters occasionally which, given how frail she was, must have taken enormous effort, but from my dad came a deafening silence. I felt really betrayed since, whenever Nathan had been in trouble in the past, I'd been the one my dad relied on to go up and sort it all out. Now suddenly I was the bad guy.

But what's that they say about time being a great healer? After Nathan had been in prison a few months, I tried again to make peace with my dad. My mother was now very ill and I knew she wouldn't live very long. I didn't want to blame my brother for the rest of my life for denying me the chance to see my mother before she died.

I wrote to my father to ask whether I could go down one weekend to see my mum. To my huge relief he agreed. That was a difficult weekend. I was happy to be reconciled with my parents but my relationship with my father had been put under enormous strain because of the attack. We tiptoed around each other for fear of bringing the whole fragile truce crumbling down around us.

My father told me that Nathan had changed in prison. He'd come off the drink and the drugs and thrown himself into educational studies and even discovered a new religious belief. Sure enough, the first time I saw my brother after the attack, at my mum's funeral, he apologised for what had happened. He seemed genuinely remorseful, genuinely reformed, back again to the vulnerable younger brother I'd always tried to look after.

Since then, the children and I visit him in prison whenever we can and he is now the one who is reaching out to us. I think he finally values his family and appreciates the love and support that is there for him. I've never talked to him about what happened during the attack when I went out of my body and watched myself lying there. Some day I imagine we'll talk about it.

It still puzzles me, and I can't explain it. All I know is that, at the point where the life was being beaten out of me, the life force within me became separated from my body and 'I' saw my physical body reaching up for it to come back.

# 9

## SAM HOLLOWAY, 35
### ENVIRONMENTAL CONSULTANT, WEST YORKSHIRE

HOW MANY TIMES has this happened to you: you're driving along, perhaps a route you've driven hundreds of times, and suddenly you realise that you haven't been concentrating, that, for the last twenty minutes or so, your mind has been elsewhere entirely? And yet you've still made it to wherever you are. You've still carried out complicated functions – changing gear, breaking, overtaking – while not in a conscious state. How does that happen? How is it that your body can do one thing while your mind is somewhere else altogether? Where, in that scenario, is the essence of you? Is it driving the car, or is it wherever your thoughts are wandering?

I believe we all have the ability to enter a different reality, a different dimension in space and time. It's just cultural conditioning that makes us try to stick a label on it – déjà vu, day-dreaming, whatever is convenient. It has taken me a long time to realise that I'm not alone in the things I've been through

– that we all experience the same states of mind; we just don't have the language to describe them.

A long time ago, I used to feel isolated from the rest of the world, but now I know that we're all connected by experience and by a myriad of invisible threads that bring us in and out of each other's lives with a series of synchronicities (or what are more often called coincidences). It has been a long journey getting to this point. It's a journey that started with a suicide and a near-death experience. But believe me in the context of my life that now seems merely incidental, a long-ago incident that kick-started a whole chain of events which has led me here.

My 'death' was really just the start…

Picture this scene. I'm fifteen. My parents are out and won't be back until the next day. My brother and I are alone in the house. Like many teenage siblings, my brother and I aren't terribly close – we're on grunting terms at best. Otherwise, we leave each other alone.

This particular night I tell him I'm going to bed early. It's not unusual – I do a milk round early in the mornings, so I often go to bed before everyone else. But something makes my brother look up. 'Are you okay?' he says out of the blue. I'm shocked. He never usually volunteers any personal questions, but he has sensed something isn't quite right.

'Yeah, fine,' I tell him, backing away.

But I am far from fine. For months, years even, feelings of isolation and anxiety have been building up inside of me. I come from a family where feelings are rarely discussed and where honour counts above all else. My father comes from a long line of soldiers. My mother, a committed Christian, is an incredibly patient woman but, like my dad, can be emotionally distant.

I'm not a boy who mixes well with other teenagers. I spend hours in the library reading books on philosophy. I worry about the state of the world. Though I have the usual teenage hormones coursing through my veins and obsessions with motorbikes and girls, you couldn't call me one of the lads.

And then there are the other mysterious things that happen to me – the times when I've seen something or heard something that I know wasn't there for other people around me.

I don't tell anyone about this for fear of being thought crazy, but it's another thing that makes me feel 'different' from everyone else. From earliest childhood, I've been aware of things – voices, images – that other people just don't hear or see. It's like background static – like having a radio on that's not quite properly tuned so you're constantly picking up other channels. Now I believe that we're all capable of picking up these kinds of messages, it's just that most of us tune them out without even being aware of what we're doing.

Anyway, this particular night I've had enough. Enough of being bullied at school and isolated at home. I can't envisage a future. This is not a cry for help. I don't want anyone to come running in to save me. I don't even want to be understood – since what I'm going through is so unique I simply don't believe that's possible. I just want to not exist any more.

I go into my bedroom and take out the bottles of sleeping pills and painkillers I've swiped from the bathroom. I've also got a bottle of vodka to wash them down with. But I find I can't really stomach the vodka, and swallow just enough to wash down the handfuls of pills.

There's a knock on my door. Amazingly, it's my brother. Again, he has the sense that something is not right and he has come to check.

'I'm fine,' I lie again, hiding the evidence. 'Just tired, that's all.'

Incredibly, in this family where so much is left unspoken, my brother doesn't take me at my word. Instead, he goes downstairs and rings my parents.

'There's something wrong,' he tells them. 'I'm sure of it.'

By the time my parents arrive, I'm feeling strange but still insist I'm fine.

'You've taken something,' says my mum seeing my wasted eyes and immediately suspecting drugs. Then she has a sudden realisation. 'Check the medicine cabinet,' she instructs my dad.

That's how they find out their son has tried to commit suicide.

I am rushed to the hospital. By the time I arrive, I am lapsing in and out of consciousness. I see smoke – hazy and white. In my head, there are weird robotic voices. I see roomfuls of people. My eyes are foggy, as though I'm peering through twilight. But there are pockets of sunshine and occasionally these illuminate some of these people, as if they're fully lit. Mainly though, they're 'shadow people'. That is, they're like negatives of people.

Where the light should be showing their features, there's shadow, obscuring immediate recognition. It's like being a child in a sunny place when people stop and bend down to talk to you and the sunlight blots out their appearance. It's as if there's a light directly behind them, so you can see their form, their stature, but not the detail. The tops of their heads are lit, edges of arms and body are shining, bridge of nose, cheeks and so on, but their faces are in shadow, especially their eyes.

I recognise the voices of some of them – they seem to be familiar, but I can't put a finger on who they are. One such

120

example has a distinctive dialect and is using phrases I recognise. I ask, 'Who are you?' and the shadow person replies, 'Don't you recognise me? It's your uncle Ben. We're all so happy to see you.'

Bizarrely, there are loads of people milling around, many seemingly unaware of me, unaware of where they are, or that the others are there. Some stand, some are sitting at tables, others walking around in small groups, pairs or even solitarily wandering. Many are old, some are young, some seem to be in period dress, as though they've just come into A & E from a fancy-dress party.

Looking back now, I get the feeling these were actually disembodied folks, maybe not ready to move on, not having realised what has happened to them. At the time, though, I just assume they are actually in the hospital, that there has been a major medical emergency sweeping the town or something. I am confused but accept what I see – as surreal or hyper-real as it seems. To say 'I see dead people' sounds a little crass now, but at the time they don't seem dead.

Only when talking with Uncle Ben do I realise they could be deceased, as Uncle Ben has been dead some time – since quite early in my childhood. It seems a little freaky, but not scary. I simply accept it, no doubt because of the effects of the overdose numbing my usual reaction pathways.

'Who are all these people?' I ask my parents.

'What people?' they reply blankly.

I am taken to have my stomach pumped. By this time, everything is folding in on itself, almost like I am in a tunnel – except the tunnel is formed by the outside edges of the world collapsing.

I see more people. Some of them are people I know. Others are total strangers. Ridiculous though it sounds, I've met quite a few of them since – others, I'm sure are waiting in the wings of my life, preparing to be introduced.

One person in particular I don't recognise at all but he keeps cropping up as if he is a major figure. I even know that his name is Rodger (I don't know anyone called Rodger at this time) and I know what he looks like as he isn't a shadow person but fully lit. For years afterwards, every time I meet someone with the name Rodger, I will take a second look, to see if he bears the face of the person from my NDE. Every time, when it turns out to be someone else who just happens to have the same name, I wonder if I will ever meet that specific Rodger from my vision. I will wonder if perhaps I am clinically schizophrenic, psychotic or otherwise simply deluded.

Then one day, an old friend turns up at my door as he is 'passing'. This is before mobile phones become the norm, so he turns up unannounced with a new acquaintance of his, who he is travelling with.

Before this new visitor can even get through the door and be formally introduced, I recognise him and say his name out loud in excitement. 'Rodger! Good to see you at last! Good to see you again,' I say.

Everyone is weirded out. Naturally, I can't explain how I know Rodger's name, never having met him before, so I just make out he reminds me of someone.

Strangely, I come to learn that this Rodger lived just a few miles from my old hometown and that we could have easily crossed paths before, as we were in the same places, around the same times, in our mutual youth. Rodger goes on to become one of my closest friends and he now knows all about how I came to know him before I met him. Stranger still, it seems he has also had some bizarre dreams and visions from his earliest memories and he, too, went through hell trying to square them with his culturally bound view of reality. We have often compared notes and have both described similar places and people in our respective visions.

There are other characters from my NDE who will become familiar to me later on. Some I know the names of, some I don't know the names of but will recognise again.

As my stomach is pumped, I have a sudden sense of elation. I feel flooded with utter calm and peace. Everything is all right. Awe is a seldom-used word but, if you ever experience it, I can assure you you'll remember it until they lower you in the box. That's how I feel. Awed. There is a melody playing, ethereal music I don't recognise.

The voices are back in my mind, but this time they're warm and friendly. 'It's not your time yet,' they tell me. 'You have other places to go, other things to do.'

The music starts to get fainter as does the sound of constant murmuring in the background, which at the beginning had seemed just like being in a room full of people locked in private yet low-key discussions – with the odd word made out, but otherwise like a chatter of sub-audible conversations.

It is as if I am walking away from this room filled with conversationalists, back down a dampening corridor towards a quiet and cosseted distant room.

When I wake up in the hospital the next day, I know that what I saw and felt the night before wasn't a dream. Nor was it a drug-induced hallucination. Like most of my generation, I've experimented a bit with illegal drugs since then, and believe me the experiences are not the same.

So real does the experience feel that I question whether that other 'death' was actually the reality, and whether my lying in the hospital bed is just a dream, a hallucination. To my mind, there's no reason anyone should have come across my suicide attempt, at least not until it was too late. What happened shouldn't have happened, not in my family at least where there are so many barriers, and where personal privacy is prized above all else.

I stay in the hospital for two days for 'observations'. The doctors and nurses don't talk a lot about my overdose but tell me that, if I hadn't been discovered when I was, I wouldn't be here right now and my family would have been distraught. 'Do you realise how serious the situation is?' they ask me. 'Do you realise what a painful death it would have been?'

Having read up on the effects of this kind of overdose, I realise that I have had a very close shave and been incredibly lucky to come back intact and without some long-term serious organ damage.

My acute embarrassment following the overdose means I don't dwell too much on what might have happened. At this time, I am still unsure whether I am actually back, or in some kind of limbo-reality or purgatory, or even still in my death throes, but living out some bizarre hallucination of what might have happened had I not been discovered by my parents.

After my suicide attempt, I feel like a failure. I have undermined my family's ethos of dignity and honour. I am ashamed and deeply embarrassed. Despite the psychologists' probing, I keep quiet about what happened. My family want to believe this was a typical adolescent cry for help. I don't tell them otherwise. My silent collusion in their version of events is the very least I can do after what I've put them through.

The taboo and shame mean that for many years I bury the experience deep within, never talking about it, denying it even to myself. I refuse to open up or try to analyse what has happened, and in time it becomes a subject that is largely unmentionable, although I still endure years of mistrust and kid-glove treatment from family and friends.

Over the next few years, I finish school, do my A levels and move on, leaving my hometown for Manchester. From the time I leave the hospital, I no longer hear or see things that no one else can. I am 'normal', I am 'cured'. I put the suicide attempt behind me and close off all memory of the near-death experience. I reinvent myself. I get a job, a girlfriend, a house. I become successful. My parents no longer watch me warily when I leave the room, or exchange meaningful looks when they think I don't see.

Though I successfully reinvent myself, I also lose something of myself in the suppression of everything that has happened. Inside I am empty, so I try to fill the void with external things – work, finding new friends, making relationships – all the exciting things in life when you're in your late teens and early twenties. To all outside appearances, I am doing A-okay. I am mercifully stable.

I forget all about the old visions and voices. I think, 'Obviously it was just in my mind, and the suicide attempt "cured" it.'

Then something happens, something that brings my near-death experience and all the memories I have suppressed sharply back into focus.

A friend – a very good, close friend – commits suicide. I am not there to save her.

This friend is my best mate's sister. She, like me, has battled with depression and suicidal thoughts. We talk endlessly about our experiences and how we've dealt with the reactions of people around us who just can't understand what it feels like. We are good for each other. Our mutual understanding of what the other has been through breaks through the longstanding isolation we've both suffered. For both of us it's the first time we don't feel alone. It's a huge and positive step forward.

Though our friendship remains platonic, we spend most of our time together. We make one another happy. Her family is over the moon to see that her life is taking off again. I think they secretly hope we will become a couple and be together forever, but neither of us wants that. It's not that kind of relationship.

Then I meet someone else – the woman who is now my wife – and things change. Inevitably, I'm not there for my friend in the way I have been before.

It's hard for her to come to terms with the fact that I can't be on call for her twenty-four hours a day like before. One day my girlfriend is ill in bed with the flu, and I feel myself coming down with the same thing. Everything aches. All I want to do is climb into bed and sleep.

But my old friend is feeling depressed. She has relapsed into old thought patterns and needs to talk. I stay up with her until 3am, trying to help her out of the depressed hole she's in, but I don't have the mental or physical energy to carry on. Deep inside, I know she's not really okay when we say our goodbyes, but I hope that she'll manage until we can carry on our chat another day. After all, we have been at these points before.

After two days, I haven't heard from her.

My best friend arrives at the house. 'She's dead,' he tells me. 'She took her own life.'

Moreover, her suicide note has mentioned me and our last discussion. Her family are stunned. They'd been convinced she was no longer suicidal. Now they can't understand how they missed the signals. I feel they blame me. Hell, I blame myself. Is there something more I could have said or done on that last night? Why didn't I make that extra effort and stay up with her?

For the next year, my life goes into meltdown. For the first time in years, I find myself thinking again of suicide. No one can reach me.

On 11 November 1993, the night before the first anniversary of her death, the visions return. It is as if my NDE has been re-triggered and I experience it all again – hearing those same voices, that melody, seeing those same figures. But, this time, I am no longer startled by the experience, but rather find it deeply emotional, full of personal meaning. For the first time, I stop trying to ignore what is being shown me or gloss over it and instead start trying to make sense of it.

This is the beginning of the change in my life, this is the catalyst. From now on, I listen to what is being told to me instead of trying to shut it out.

Finally, all these years later, I've begun to understand what it all means and what it has all been about in terms of how we live and how we die.

There's a taboo surrounding death. It's spooky, it's contradictory, it's the unknown. Only by wiping it from our radar can we function effectively in our ordinary day-to-day lives. Instead, we bury ourselves in the minutiae of life, unwilling to look at the bigger picture. We've all become disconnected from meaning in our lives, from any kind of moral framework.

One of the things I've learned from my NDE, from what has been conveyed to me and the whole experience of my life, is that we have to connect to one another again, and to a sense of the common good. For the future of the planet, we have to start looking outside of our individual boxes and seeing the global picture.

It has been hard for me to open up to people about what I've experienced and understood. There's a resistance to anything that takes people out of their comfort zones and makes them confront bigger questions. I've been with my wife for fourteen years, but it took a while before I told her what had been going on. And even then I made her promise beforehand not to write me off as 'crazy' (luckily, she is open-minded and willing to listen without judging).

And yet, I'm not alone in having seen what I've seen or known what I've known. I think there's a general movement now in the UK towards an understanding that we've all got a lot more going on under the surface than we know. I think all of us are looking to find a connection to the infinite within us. You don't have to have an NDE to realise all this stuff – there are many paths to the same destination.

I'm not saying I know the answers to everything that bothered me before, just that it's important to ask the questions.

My own life has come full circle since my near-death experience. I have a son who is now three and, incredible though it still seems, we've moved back to my hometown. In fact, we're living in my father's house, which I know is going to sound very biblical, but was never intended that way! Moving back here, I had a lot of demons to face, with regard to my suicide attempt, which was the event that drove me away in the first place. But I'm getting there.

I've made a lot of changes to my life. I've taken a big drop in income in order to go freelance as an environmental consultant. It has meant financial sacrifices but I have to put my money where my mouth is, so to speak, by investing something in making things better for future generations. And the great thing about it is that I get to spend time at home watching my son grow up.

I've built a lot of bridges with my own family and it means a great deal to see my son growing up connected to his grandparents. When I moved back, my father found a box in the attic that was crammed with old notebooks and schoolbooks from when I was a child. I hadn't thought anything had survived from that time. Looking through my English books, I found stories in there I'd written based on the perceptions and visions I'd had as a child. 'Very imaginative,' the teachers had written time after time. And yet, these weren't from my imagination. These were actual experiences.

At that time I didn't know what to do with them, couldn't cope with the responsibility of being 'different'. That's what led to the suicide attempt and the NDE. Now things have changed. I've changed. And I'm determined to make up for the mistakes of the past, by building something positive for the future.

# 10
## GLORIA GUNN, 65
### FARMER, CORNWALL

SOMETIMES YOU'LL HAVE an experience that seems so strange and unique you keep it to yourself convinced that no one else will be able to make sense of it. Then some time later – maybe months or even years – you'll hear a chance remark, a throwaway comment, and you'll think, 'But that's exactly what happened to me!' And what was deeply personal suddenly becomes part of something bigger, a wider phenomenon.

This is how it was with my NDE.

It was December 1965 and I was in labour with my first child, my son Duncan. I was at home. In those days, home births were considered quite okay as long as you were a fit young woman and had hot and cold running water. I was twenty-five and in fine health so there didn't seem to be any particular risks. In attendance were the midwife and my ex-husband Roy, who was considerably more scared than me.

The birth was reasonably straightforward, but obviously

painful and very tiring. The third stage in particular seemed to drag on and on in a blur of effort and agony. I'd had a small injection of pethadine early on in the labour to help control the pain but by this stage it was wearing off and the minutes seemed to tick by with excruciating slowness.

By the time Duncan finally made his appearance, I was exhausted, but also hugely excited and relieved that he was okay. Well, perfect really.

It was after that when things started to go wrong. While the placenta was being delivered, I started to haemorrhage. As the blood poured out, the midwife tried vainly to stop it, soaking up towel after towel.

Then suddenly I was aware that I wasn't on the bed any more. I was somewhere up above, near the ceiling, looking down on what was happening. I was neither frightened nor happy, just mildly curious, watching the midwife and Roy scurrying around fetching towel after towel.

I remember feeling faintly puzzled as I surveyed the scene, wondering what on earth was going on. I could see an outline on the bed and I thought, 'My goodness, that's me!' But I couldn't see myself in any kind of detail – just a shrouded shape in the bed.

The midwife wasn't panicking. She was just getting on with the task of trying to clean up the blood, but Roy didn't seem to really know what to do with himself.

I didn't feel anything watching them going about their business; the only sensation floating through my mind was that vague curiosity. It was neither pleasant nor unpleasant. I didn't see a light, I didn't go through a tunnel, I just watched what was going on.

And then it was over. One minute I was up on the ceiling, the next I was back in my body, drifting in and out of consciousness.

Later, I learned I'd lost a huge amount of blood. When the doctor arrived to check me over, I heard the midwife whispering about the haemorrhage and just how much blood I'd lost. But I didn't go to hospital. In those days, women just got on with it really.

Later I told Roy that I'd had a 'curious experience'. I didn't really explain it in any detail, and he couldn't help me piece anything together because, apparently, as the haemorrhage went on, he'd passed out, unable to bear the sight of all that blood.

Other than that, I didn't tell anyone else what had happened. It just seemed too improbable. Then, a few years later, I was listening to the radio and I heard someone describing exactly the same experience I'd had.

I can't remember exactly what I was doing, but I know I sat up and thought, 'Good Lord, that's what happened to me.'

I still don't know how to explain my experience. I know it wasn't a dream or a hallucination. It felt real and is as clear today as if it just happened. It hasn't faded like a dream or changed in any way.

It wasn't a particularly dramatic NDE as far as they go, but it has had a big effect on me. I'm not frightened of dying. I'm slightly put off by the physical process of it, but death itself holds no sting. I wouldn't like to tell other people what to believe but I have a private view that something of us stays on after death – some essence that is never destroyed.

That view was reinforced a few years after my NDE by what happened to my father. He was a real down-to-earth East Ender. He didn't talk much about feelings and certainly wasn't one for spirituality. But, six months before he died, he told me a curious story.

It was 19 September 1970 and he was woken up by the sound of his mother's voice calling him. Instinctively, he glanced at the alarm clock he always kept by the bed and saw it was exactly midnight. He'd been with his mother when she died and it was twenty-five years to the day and even the minute from when she'd taken her last breath.

When he told me about this, it was so out of character, I shivered.

'What a good thing you didn't reply, Dad,' I said without thinking.

My father himself died six months later but, irrationally, I was convinced that, if he'd replied to his mother's voice calling that night, he'd have gone there and then.

That fits in with what I think now about death and dying. I don't see death as an end. I don't mean to say I know what happens, but I do know the lines are very much more blurred than that.

For me, that's quite comforting.

# 11

## HARRY HONE, 91
### WRITER AND PUBLISHER, NORTH VIRGINIA, USA

ON WEDNESDAY, 15 December 1976, I had retired for the night after what had been a usual kind of day. I looked the same as I usually looked, and felt the same as I usually felt. Usual, normal – and ready for a night's sleep. Then, at four o'clock on the morning of 16 December, something very unusual and abnormal took place.

I had awakened from a deep sleep and walked to the bathroom, a distance of some twenty feet. Then from nowhere, and with breathtaking suddenness, I received what felt like a vicious kick in the chest. It was as if an elephant had stomped on my ribs. The breath left my body and I became weak and limp, and fell to the floor.

I clutched at my heart in a futile effort to ward off the next assault. This came in the form of a slow but relentless kind of torture. It seemed as though a huge steel vice had been fastened on my heart, and a giant with superhuman strength was squeezing the life out of me. Powerless to resist or escape from the torture, and with what seemed like the last breath I would ever take, I called out to my wife, 'Lou, please help me.'

Miraculously, she heard my barely audible voice, and flew to my rescue. Within seconds, I felt her warm hands massaging my heart through the walls of my chest.

Under the influence of her loving care and warm words of concern, I regained some measure of confidence. The excruciating pain began to evaporate as she continued with instinctive but untutored first aid.

I was unable to speak, but voicelessly conveyed my gratitude through my eyes. I am convinced that her prompt action in those first early moments saved my life. As she continued her attempts at first aid, I began to breathe more rhythmically – but still very shallowly.

The agony inflicted on my heart from that 'one–two' assault slowly faded, only to be replaced with cold, shivering sweats. Lou told me later that my face was ashen grey. She was scared and puzzled, but bravely kept her composure.

Though these events happened back in 1976, I'll never forget how it felt to be lying there helpless on the floor. To me, Lou represented life itself. We'd been everything to one another since getting married in Gretna Green decades before after a secret elopement when I was twenty-two and she nineteen. Together we'd raised our three children and survived the traumatic move from England to the USA. My deepest desire was to hang on to her – and I prayed for the strength to do so.

As the colour slowly came back to my face, and I began to feel and look more 'alive', she decided she could risk leaving me in order to call the doctor. It was now almost 4.30, and within thirty minutes our local doctor made his appearance. My wife quickly gave him the details of my sudden collapse, and he examined me right where I lay on the bathroom floor. His verdict, in concerned but certain tones, was that I had suffered a heart attack. Leaving me lying prone where I had fallen, he called the rescue squad.

I was a very passive spectator. Still too weak to move or even speak, my mind was alertly conscious of what was going on around me. By the time the ambulance arrived, some strength had returned to my body, and I could talk.

This was progress. I felt the worst was over. As the 45-minute ride to Riverside Hospital in Newport News brought me closer to more organised medical help, I mentally noted that the ambulance needed new springs – or the road needed repairs. I marvelled at the irrelevance of my thought processes, and patiently resigned myself to what would happen next.

I didn't have long to wait.

Once inside the hospital emergency ward, doctors appeared like magic. With professional speed and attention, they carried out further medical checks. In answers to their questioning, I gave them the same account of the sequence of events my wife had given the local GP. As I recounted the details, I had the distinct impression I was talking about something that had happened to someone else.

Everything seemed to be so unreal and impossible. I had heard of other people having heart attacks – but never once dreamed it could possibly happen to me.

Still in the emergency room, the doctors left me under the care of a nurse. This gave me a respite from further questions and a chance to collect my scattered thoughts.

At this point my wife arrived. For a few moments we held hands. I felt safe again. However, we were interrupted by the arrival of still another physician who asked me to sign some official-looking papers. Immediately after this matter of protocol was over, I was propelled into the Cardiac Care Unit.

I made the transition from a mobile stretcher into an immobile bed without mishap. An attentive nurse took my blood pressure, and I was wired to an electrocardiograph.

Later, I was asked still more questions. As I responded I became aware that not only was I the victim of the attack, I was also the raconteur.

As a new patient in the Cardiac Care Unit, instructions were given to me as to what I could and couldn't do. I was told to press the red button if I needed immediate help. To be perfectly frank, I was only remotely aware of these verbal orders. At this point, I still felt tired and battered. However, my wife informed me I did look a little better.

In the usual run of things, visitors were allowed a ten-minute stay with the patients. By this time, however, Lou had been at my bedside about four hours. The entire staff at Riverside Hospital was professionally attentive and wonderfully understanding. After a conference with the attending physicians, Lou advised me she would have to leave in order that I could have complete rest. I was disappointed, but felt relieved when she told me she'd be back again in a couple of hours or so.

She kissed me gently – and left.

It was now about 11am. I had been in the hospital approximately five hours.

Then, at 11.27am, it happened.

I can recall the circumstances clearly. First, I began to feel nauseated, and tried to sit up in bed. I succeeded in doing this, but immediately began to feel worse. I became awfully weak – and felt myself slipping away. It didn't feel at all like fainting. Fainting feels like giving up. This felt like being taken away.

I got the impression I was leaving on a journey to an unknown destination. I felt sure I was going somewhere else. With my last breath, I called out, 'Something is wrong – I am going.' And I went.

I discovered later that the patient in the adjacent bed had called out to the attending nurses. Two of them immediately rushed to my bedside. The doctors weren't far behind.

The medical terminology for their concern was described as a 'cardiac arrest'. In other words, my heart had stopped beating. I had left for a brief visit to another world – and what I saw there would change my life.

At the moment of my 'departure' from my physical self, I felt myself being pulled away from the here and now and propelled at lightning speed into what I can only describe as the future.

The power that pulled me was irresistible and, strangely enough, I had no desire to resist. I went completely willingly.

The force that controlled the direction of my journey was delightfully persuasive. I actually found myself excited about my journey and looking forward to my arrival at my final destination. Its gentle pulsating power guided me firmly and unerringly into a tunnel-like black void where, in spite of the impenetrable darkness, I found I could see.

I had the feeling that I was still me – but without the inertia and weight of my physical body. My body was 'there' and I was 'here'. I became acutely aware of the separation. At the same time, I felt wondrously at peace, and had an almost euphoric anticipation as to what I might see next. As I said before, all was dark in the tunnel — yet I could see. It was at that moment I realised that I myself was the light that enabled me to see. And, at the end of the tunnel, I emerged into an indescribable pure white world of light.

When I looked back where I'd come from, I could see my body lying on the hospital bed surrounded by doctors and nurses. They were working feverishly, trying to induce me to come back. In a detached but still interested way, I saw all this from a vantage point outside my body. They were frantic — I was calm. They were in 'this' world — I was in the 'other'.

In my conscious but apparently invisible state, I knew I was still *in* the world — but not *of* it. I saw everything that was going on without being an active and recognisable participant. It was something like being at the movies. I could see the actors playing their parts as though from a seat in a darkened cinema. I could see them — but it was obvious they couldn't see me. They were completely oblivious to my presence, and were totally immersed in the world I had just left. They were desperately trying to bring me back.

But just as in a cinema there has to be a projectionist, making all the action possible, so I became very much aware that the scene I was watching was dependent on some other external force that I couldn't see. Before a movie starts, the man in the booth switches on the light. Without the shaft of light, nothing is visible — nothing exists. When I looked down at my body lying on the bed, there was no movement at all. The light was missing. In my new environment, I came to the instant realisation that I — the me that now only existed in this other world — was the light that made moving pictures possible.

I think that's why it was easy to distance myself from that physical body. The light that had made me 'me' wasn't there any more. I believe the same thing happens to us all when our time comes to die. The light will go out, you'll leave your body and, for a moment if you look, you'll still see it lying there. Then, with a final glance, you will leave it forever. Your need for a physical body has ended.

If you decided to leave your house for the last time, you would probably snap off the light before you left, and, if the furnace were on, you'd turn that off, too. Like your body, your house would become empty, dark and soon grow cold.

On your way out, you might also walk down the garden path to the gate. Once there, you might decide to take one last final look at the house you had lived in for so many years.

It would still be there, right where you had left it, but 'you' wouldn't be inside – you'd be on the outside looking in.

That's exactly what it's like when you leave your body. You will probably turn around to take one last look at it – like I did. It will still be there, inert and lifeless. It would appear very much as it does when you are sleeping – but there would be a distinct difference.

'You' are not in residence. 'You' have left. Your body, like your house, is empty. Its temporary resident has moved out for the last time. You will return to where you came from. Your body will return to where *it* came from.

In that moment, I learned that leaving the body is the perfectly natural thing to do.

If the house you lived in had deteriorated so badly that the roof continually leaked, or the foundations were crumbling, or the walls were collapsing, you'd move out as quickly as possible.

If your house was sound, but a sudden annihilating accident occurred and ripped it apart, you'd still vacate it at the first opportunity. Then, having moved out – but still needing a place to live – you'd retreat to an area of safety until another house was ready for you to occupy.

The same happens to your physical body when you die. It's old, it's worn out, it has been involved in an 'accident' or the 'lease' has run out or it has been claimed by disease. 'Dis-ease' is exactly what the word implies. 'You' are not at ease in your 'house'. So you move out.

Where do you go? Well, my experience shows me, you go back to the place where you came from before you moved in. You go to where 'God' is. This is the same place from which you originated. Some people call it the 'body of Christ'. If by 'Christ' they mean 'light', then the word is an exact one, and is interchangeable with 'God'.

Before I died on that fateful morning of 16 December, I hadn't been a particularly religious man. I'd never been a member of any denominational church, although, being English, I was a nominal Episcopalian.

During my life, I had attended services at both Protestant and Catholic churches in and around London where I grew up. As a child, I attended Sunday School and had earned a book full of golden stars for regular attendance. It was there my ideas about church and Christianity were formed. The memories and impressions of those early years in Sunday School are vivid ones. I remember them in all their clarity to this day.

As a result of my 'dying' experience and my confused beliefs before this event, I am now convinced these teachings were largely fairy tales.

During my timeless journey into darkness and light, the truth I so desperately wanted to discover as a child was revealed to me in a sudden blaze of instant knowledge. I was no longer listening to the theories and fantasies of people who hadn't been there. I saw the truth exactly.

I found God where He said He was – in the darkness of that long black tunnel, or void. He expressed Himself to me as an indescribable white light. He was, in truth, the light at the end of the tunnel.

And the incredible thing was that I was also an integral part of that indescribable white light. I was aware that God was with me. I didn't arrive at this awareness by hearing words. Instead, the realisation of the truth and the answers to my questions of a lifetime simply became part of my consciousness in the twinkling of an eye.

In the beginning, as I've already described, all was dark and void. This was the long dark tunnel I travelled through to eventually find the light. (As did many others who have made the same journey and reported the same experience.) When I emerged into the light, it truly was indescribable and filled with peace and joy. Without words being spoken, I was made aware of many things.

I learned there is no such thing as life and death. There is only life – and that is Life Eternal. Just as we sleep between one day and the next, so we 'sleep' between one life and the next.

As far as you are concerned, the world exists only for as long as you are in it. When I died, I entered a new dimension. The world of the here and now no longer existed. When you die, the light will go out, all will be dark and void, and everything you now perceive as 'real' will disappear. Reality cannot exist without consciousness. When we no longer have the capacity to imagine, there is no world. The instant my heart stopped, I began my journey into the other dimension. By earthly time standards, I wasn't away very long. The nurse who beat on my chest to bring me back said I was only 'gone' for a couple of minutes. It could very well have been only a couple of seconds. Time was not important.

For example, during the short time I was 'dead' and in this other world of darkness and light, my entire life flashed before me. It was just like an authentic replay of one of those *This is Your Life* television programmes. There was no screen title, credits or musical score. It began with startling suddenness with the very first frame and flashed across the screen of my vision — from birth to death — in the twinkling of an eye.

I was shown the 'highlights' of my life — the times when I increased the totality of my share of the light, and the times I diminished it.

I first saw the place and the house of my birth. In real life, I had never seen or visited it. It was in Birmingham, England. I was 'told' to make a pilgrimage there. After my recovery, this was one of the first things I did.

In 'this' world, I had often complained that the life I had lived was not the life I had envisioned for myself. During and after the replay sequences, I could see clearly that it was.

True enough, I had wanted certain things — but I also saw I had actually 'imaged' something else. In asking and praying for a happy and successful life, I saw that I repeatedly doubted the outcome of my prayers. In other words, I wanted something in my mind but, beset with doubt, I imaged something entirely different.

That retrospective instant replay of my life emphasised one

dominant theme – that the imagination is the place where all things begin. If you 'image' something, and then develop the image, your life will reflect the picture.

In the Bible it says, 'as ye sow ye shall reap'. If you merely sow the seed of the image and do nothing to develop it, it will remain as nothing more than a figment of your imagination. It will have no roots and will never bloom. Starting to develop an image and then allowing it to wither on the vine as a result of doubts or fears that it really will grow had been the reason for all my 'failures'.

As my past life unfolded, I was not consciously aware of time limitations. The life I saw flashing past me was just as real, just as long and just as solid as the life I had recently left behind.

Though my body was still on the hospital bed where I had left it, the body I was watching now was far more dynamic and alive, and I saw it growing from childhood into adulthood with every detail included – many of which I had completely forgotten.

When the flashback sequences of my life were over, the next series of experiences took place. They seemed like revelations. What I saw and heard at this junction was in direct response to my searching questions.

I was programmed with an avalanche of new knowledge, and given a number of missions to complete, including one to find my sister Dulcie, whom I'd lost touch with thirty-four years before.

At this stage in the experience, I was also made aware that I'd be allowed a degree of pre-vision when I returned to life.

After acquiring this knowledge, I was 'told' I would have to go back and was abruptly brought back to this world of substance, the world we have come to accept as the 'real' world. I was reluctant to leave. Contrary to all our beliefs, I'd found the process of death to be a delightful experience and the place of death to be one of absolute peace.

The first thing I saw on my return was what appeared to be an angel. However, unlike any angel I had ever heard of, this one was beating in a most un–angelic way on my chest with her fists. The angel was a nurse. Her name, I learned later, was Eileen Smith. I don't suppose I will ever forget her name. Another 'angel' was about to give me artificial resuscitation by means of a plastic mouthpiece. This was another nurse. The first words I heard came from her: 'Thank God I've got him back; thank God I've got him back.'

At this moment, I knew I had returned. Like the nurse said, I had come 'back'.

If I could have spoken at that moment, I would have said 'thank God' too. Since speaking was impossible with a plastic mouthpiece in the way, I brought up my hand and brushed it away. I remember it flying across the room and landing on the floor with a loud click.

I became aware there were several people gathered round my bed. The cardiologists in attendance and both nurses looked relieved. I felt somewhat bewildered. I tried to convey my thanks through my eyes. Once again, I found myself breathless and physically weak. However, my mental processes seemed as alert as ever and, while I lay there recovering from my experiences, I started to try to put all the jumbled pieces together.

Fortunately, my visit to the 'other world' had been brief, but I will always remember the scenery. In the brief passage of time I was away, I discovered there are two worlds. The world of the senses and that of the spirit. 'Spirit' is a poor choice of words, but I can't think of any other word to use. All I can say is that, whatever word is used, it is pitifully inadequate to describe the world we all go to when we die.

It was the consensus of the physicians who examined me prior to and during my journey into the beyond that I had suffered another heart attack. I had felt excruciating pain, my heart stopped, and only heroic efforts to get me back had got it beating again.

Normally, that diagnosis would entail a lifetime of medication and vastly increased risk of future heart failure. But while I was in the 'other world' – and again when I came back – I prayed for a complete healing. I prayed that my heart would be restored and returned to perfect and normal functioning.

Incredibly, it was.

I was discharged from intensive care in three days and was out of the hospital in less than five. Subsequent examinations by the cardiologists who monitored me throughout my stay in the hospital could find no traces of a heart attack or any effects from the cardiac arrest. The consultant, in whom I had complete confidence, said it was a unique case. In fact, immediately prior to discharge, my treadmill-test performance was more like that of an athlete than a heart patient. My wife was delighted and astonished. I was, as you'd imagine, thankful beyond words. When I was in the light, I'd been told I'd be granted a 'measure of immortality'. Well, believe what you will, but I'm ninety-one now and still in the best of health.

After returning home, the pre-visions started, just as I'd been told they would.

The first one of these pre-visions involved the horrendous tragedy of Toccoa Falls in Northeastern Georgia. This was the Bible college where a number of students and faculty were swept away to their deaths by the sudden collapse of the Toccoa Dam.

Twenty-four hours before the disaster occurred, I 'saw' it happen in all its pent-up fury. I saw the dam shudder, heard the thunderous noise and then saw the raging torrent sweep down the Falls and wash away everything it met in its path.

With tears in my eyes, I described the scene to my wife. Since I was sleeping in bed at the time I witnessed these events, we both concluded it must have been a 'nightmare'. The newspapers and television news the next evening told us otherwise. The disaster had occurred exactly as I had 'seen' it.

I also undertook the missions I'd been charged with. The most pleasurable of these – one which had seemed almost impossible at the time – was the discovery of my sister Dulcie. While I was dead, I'd asked how I could find her. Along with my other questions, I was programmed with the answer and did exactly what I was programmed to do at the time I was programmed to do it.

Despite not having had word of Dulcie for more than three decades, I wrote to the *Courier Mail* newspaper in Brisbane, Australia, telling them of my mission and enclosing a photograph of Dulcie and myself taken more than thirty-five years earlier while I was serving in the Royal Air Force. They generously printed my appeal. The response was instantaneous. A cable from Dulcie was followed by a telephone call that effectively ended the vacuum of silence and separation. My prayers had been answered – Dulcie was found. I believe that happened simply because I believed it was possible.

Even though I've now lived through nine decades, I harbour absolutely no fears about dying. During my brief stay in that other world, I developed a deep love for it that I will always find difficult to explain.

It was a welcome release from the trauma of what we call real life. You can take my word for it, this world as we live it is a battleground on which we fight an unending war. The other world is the place where we find the 'peace that passeth all understanding'.

I should know – I've been there.

# 12

## KATE JOHNSON, 60
### FILM MAKER, LONDON

SITTING IN THE doctor's waiting room, I picked up the nearest magazine to hand. It was the *News of the World* supplement – not something I'd ever normally read – and I started flicking idly through it. I was feeling really impatient – I'm not the most patient of people at the best of times – and so wasn't really taking in what I was reading. I was just wishing the doctor would jolly well hurry up so I could get on with all the other things I had to do that day.

Still with half a mind on other things, I started reading one of the features. I forget what it was called, but it had the words 'near-death experience' somewhere near the top. As I was reading, I became more and more engrossed, forgetting for once about the fact that I'd been waiting for ages and was going to be late for whatever I had to do next. The people in the magazine article were talking about how they'd nearly died and come back to life, how they'd seen tunnels and lights.

'My God,' I thought to myself. 'That's what happened to *me!*'

For the first time in years, I found myself thinking back to that time in the South of France and to the accident. But this time I was looking at everything in a new light. Now I had a name for what I'd gone through.

It was Easter Sunday 1990 and I was holidaying in Cannes with my seven-year-old daughter, Sammy, and my friend Carole and her daughter, Izzie. Carole and Izzie were on the beach but Sammy and I had gone back to our fourth-floor apartment and were sitting on the balcony enjoying the sun. From where we sat, we had an uninterrupted view across the busy seafront road to the beach and the sea beyond.

It had been getting slightly breezy that morning and all of a sudden a freak gust of wind swept over the balcony, carrying cassettes and chair cushions with it, right over the balustrade and across the road, ending up on the opposite pavement.

'Mummy's just going to go and get all our stuff,' I told Sammy. Then, not bothering to change out of my vest and bikini bottoms (I was a lot thinner then!), I made my way downstairs, having locked the front door of the apartment.

I crossed the road without a problem and picked up the bits and pieces belonging to us, to the amusement of the passers-by. Then I started to cross the road back towards the apartment. The traffic was quite heavy and I waited until a coach kindly stopped for me. That's the last thing I remember. Apparently, as I started to cross, a young dude with three girls in his car came up behind the coach and, without stopping to think 'I wonder why it's stopped' like any normal person, overtook it on the blindside to me.

I don't remember anything about the impact when he hit me or about flying through the air and landing with a thud by the side of the road. Carole and Izzie heard the commotion from the beach.

'Mum, I think something's happened to Kate,' Izzie apparently said, without even having looked. It was just a feeling she had, she told me later.

By the time they arrived at the roadside, the ambulance was there and I'd been covered in blankets from head to toe. My poor daughter, who'd been watching the whole scene from the balcony of our flat, remembers this as being the most terrifying thing – that shroud of blankets they made me.

I was rushed to hospital, where frantic doctors tried to find out the extent of my head and leg injuries. But I knew nothing about all that. In my mind, I was somewhere else entirely.

The next memory I have after starting to cross the road is of being in a tunnel with lots of mad moving colours. I was falling through the air. It was like those dreams you used to have as a child where you're just falling, falling, falling and you wake up with a real start. Everything felt all over the place and I felt very disorientated.

Then suddenly the colours sorted themselves out into a pattern and I was in a giant kaleidoscope. That's when I relaxed and realised it was rather nice to be falling freely through all these amazing beautiful patterns. When I was a child, I was fascinated by kaleidoscopes and would look through them for hours on end, mesmerised by the changing colours. Now I was actually inside one just falling weightlessly down without a care in the world.

But just as I thought this, I realised I did have a care. 'I'm a mother,' I remembered.

I don't know where that thought came from but, once I had it in my mind, I couldn't stop thinking about it. All my life I've had this fear about mothers being separated from their children. I remember taking my nieces to see a film about a bear cub who lost his mother and they were mortified because I was crying so loudly. I think it stems from the fact that my mother lost her own first-born child early on, and it gave me a lifelong fear about the fragility of family relationships – that any moment you could lose that protection and unconditional love that a mother gives her child.

Falling through the kaleidoscope tunnel, I thought of my daughter, still locked in the apartment. Who would help her? I knew I had to get back to save her.

'I'm not ready to go,' I realised.

As soon as that thought occurred to me, I saw a bright dot of white light ahead of me. It hadn't been there before. It was as if my thinking about my daughter had conjured it up.

Up until this moment, I hadn't wanted to stop falling. It felt so nice and relaxing. But now, I made a conscious effort to stop free-falling and move towards the white dot. I can't explain how I did it, I just kind of tensed my muscles and moved myself mentally in the direction of the light. As I did so, it started getting bigger and bigger.

And then I burst back into consciousness. I really can't think of another way of putting it. One second I was heading towards the bright light and the next I was waking up with a French doctor sewing up my head.

'Où est ma fille?' I asked.

I spoke in French, not because I'd remembered I was in France, but because I'd been reading Lawrence Durrell's novel *The Alexandria Quartet* that morning. In my mind I was in Alexandria, the Egyptian city steeped in French culture and language.

The doctor was relieved, but shocked, to find this comatose woman suddenly wide awake and barking questions at him. He tried to explain about the accident and that I'd fractured my skull and my left fibula, but I wasn't really taking it in. The injury to my head was making me feel really dizzy and disorientated. The doctor insisted on showing me how close I'd come to being dead – he got my little finger and measured out half of the width of my nail between his own finger and thumb. That had been the distance between life and death for me – one eighth of an inch. If my head had hit the ground just that fraction further round to the right, I wouldn't have survived.

I had my leg put in plaster from the hip to the foot and was taken to a geriatric ward, which was terrible – full of old ladies in great pain. All I could think of was Sammy, but they wouldn't let her come in to see me. Carole came to visit, looking more shaken than me. She told me Sammy was fine, but I was confused and shaken and I wouldn't believe her. After she'd gone, I dragged myself out of bed and literally crawled out into the corridor to the public phone.

'Oh, Mummy, I thought you'd have lost your memory and forgotten I was your very own daughter,' Sammy cried when she heard my voice on the phone.

Those are the exact words she said, I'll never forget it. In fact, even talking about it now all these years later, I've got tears in my eyes – 'your very own daughter'. What a funny thing to say.

I stayed in the French hospital in that horrible geriatric ward with the groaning old women for another three days before friends insisted on moving me to the American hospital. Doctors there performed a brain scan and found that, thank goodness, there was no permanent damage.

Finally, about eight days after my accident, I was taken by ambulance to the airport to fly back to the UK. I've never felt quite so vulnerable. I was deposited in a wheelchair, with only Sammy to look after me, and left to wait for hours while the plane was delayed. Then, when it was finally ready to leave, I realised they expected me to walk up the steps to get inside.

'You must be joking,' I said, indicating my leg, still in plaster from thigh to foot and my throbbing head with its comedy bandage.

But no, they weren't joking. I'll never know where I found the strength to haul myself up those steps and on to the plane.

Back in London, the recovery began. My leg was badly broken and, it later transpired, my kneecap had been cracked. As this wasn't picked up on at the time, it has caused me a lot of problems over the years and I still have trouble walking long distances and climbing steps.

I was also left with terrible vertigo that made me pass out all the time. I couldn't drive and had to hire someone to take me around.

One of the things that can happen when you survive something like that is that you become very depressed, which is what happened to me. I'd recently split up with my husband, Sammy's father, and had given up a lovely life with a housekeeper and a chauffeur in order to get involved with a man who had no intention of committing to me, so it was a difficult time personally.

But there was also this feeling of 'why me?' I couldn't work out why I'd been allowed to come back, what the bigger plan was for my life. And I became intensely upset at the thought that I'd missed my chance to die rather a nice, kind sort of death.

There one minute, gone the next. No pain, no nothing. What if, the next time, I got really ill and lingered on in agony? What if I died a slow painful death?

Luckily, I had Sammy to look after because she kept me from sinking too far into the black hole of depression and, gradually, little by little, I came out of it.

I stopped thinking, 'Why have I been given another chance?' and started to think, 'I just have, that's all.' It was pointless to keep speculating, I had to start living again. I started asking myself questions about what it is I really wanted to do with my life. One of my big regrets had always been not going to college, so I decided to apply and to my amazement got accepted on a course to study screenwriting and documentary film-making.

This opened up a whole new world to me, and I've worked in film and television ever since graduating. So, in a sense, my near-death experience did change my life in that I made decisions I might otherwise not have done, and really sorted out my priorities.

But I wouldn't like to give the idea that I think about it all the time. I look on it as just another experience I survived and lived through, in a whole lifetime of extraordinary experiences.

I'm a great believer in the idea that things happen when they're supposed to and nothing happens by accident. I think my experience in the kaleidoscope tunnel was my consciousness taking off somewhere else, and I believe it was meant to knock some sense back into me about my priorities in life, after having left my marriage and being in this kind of limbo.

I still worry about what's in store for me the next time I 'die'. I've always been a very fit person, which is why I survived the accident so well, and my great fear is of having a long-term illness. I don't think I could bear it. But I don't have any fear of death itself. It's nice. It's easy.

# 13

## SUZY WALTERS, 23
### TRAINEE TEACHER, BALTIMORE, USA

IT WAS SATURDAY, 6 March 2004 and I was getting ready to go out. To be honest, I didn't really want to go. It would have been so easy just to stay in and watch TV or sleep, slobbing around in my oldest clothes, just as I normally did. But some friends had invited me out to see a show and I knew I should make the effort.

For some unknown reason, I dressed with real care. Where I live, most people just throw on a pair of jeans to go out, but, on this occasion, I put on my best green floral dress, some boots and a necklace, as if I was going out to meet someone really special. In a strange way, that's exactly what I did. Because, later that night, I met my best, oldest, dearest friend – Joel. Nothing odd about that, you might think, except that he'd been dead for nearly a year.

I think that's why my friends were so keen to get me out that night. Because the next day, 7 March, would have been Joel's

159

birthday – the first since he'd died. They didn't want me moping around on my own, thinking about him. I didn't tell them that I thought about him all the time, no matter where I was.

Joel and I had gone to the same junior school, a strict Christian school in Maryland, Baltimore. We were both very shy and didn't really become close friends until he was in the ninth grade and I was in the tenth. That was when we slowly discovered we had a lot in common. We did drama together, and we both liked to draw. Although I couldn't play any instruments like he could, we shared a real love of music. We would take trips together to record stores, getting excited by the same things. We also had the same sense of style. Together we'd comb the second-hand shops for unusual clothes, and I took up sewing so I could make things for him and me. We created our own little world. I was very supportive of his bands, and he was very supportive of my artwork. We admired each other's talents, but also had a certain amount of jealousy and competitiveness, secretly measuring ourselves against one another.

Our relationship was hard to define. We shared kisses in high school but then one time he confessed that he thought he might be gay. Then days later he'd be kissing me again. Needless to say, it was a confusing time – but that's what growing up is all about. I always knew that, whatever happened, Joel treasured our friendship and, even when he had girlfriends or I had boyfriends, we stayed very close. That's what was most important to me.

It was a few years into our friendship that the differences between us started to show. Joel and I both had younger brothers. We all loved to sit around the table and laugh and share stories. But, while my brother was into soccer, Joel's got into drugs. My parents were still together and very supportive of me, but Joel's dad was never home and his parents eventually got divorced while he was in his last year of secondary school.

Eventually, I went off to college while Joel stayed home. The first college I went to was okay and I made friends, but I wasn't really happy and decided to move to somewhere closer to home. I was accepted into two colleges but chose the one closest to Joel. He was going through a really hard time and I wanted to be there for him.

Joel's parents were both getting remarried, and Joel had become convinced that his father hated him. At the same time his brother was going more off the rails — he'd been thrown out of school and was still doing drugs.

Though Joel had dated a lot of girls without getting seriously hurt, he became involved with an older woman at around this time.

'I'm in love,' he told me, his eyes shining.

As soon as he told me that, I froze. I just knew she was going to break his heart. When she broke up with him a few months later, true enough she left him with a broken heart — and a serious cocaine habit.

Joel went into a complete decline. He felt like he was alone and everyone else was moving on except for him. He was really hurting and had very few people to turn to.

In March 2003, a short time after he split from his girlfriend, Joel and I were out when he began throwing up violently. In my naivety, I assumed he'd had too much to drink so I took him home and put him to bed.

'It's okay,' I told him, stroking his head. 'Everyone has bad days from time to time. Everything will be all right.'

Later, his friends told me he'd taken heroin for the first time that night but at that stage I had no idea his drug taking had got so extreme.

In May 2003, he showed up at my apartment.

'I'm in a bad way,' he told me. 'I desperately need somewhere to stay.'

Of course, I said 'yes' — it wouldn't have occurred to me not to. One night soon after he arrived, we slept together. We'd never gone as far as that before, but Joel was really needy. I didn't really want to sleep with him — I knew he was using the intimacy like a drug to take the edge off his pain. But I loved him, and I didn't know what else to do.

'I never slept with you before because I was so scared of losing you as a friend,' I told him.

'You'll never lose me,' he said fiercely.

Joel swore to me that he'd stopped using the drugs. That was part of the deal for him living with me — that it would give him an opportunity to clean himself up. I was young and naive about these things and wanted desperately to believe him.

We fell into a pattern whereby I almost became his mother. Every night I put him to bed, much as I had that night he'd been sick, patting his head and reassuring him about almost everything. On bad nights, I'd get him a drink of water, or medicine to help him sleep.

When he'd been there a couple of weeks, I had to go away for a few days. My flatmate, Stacy, was really depressed — her younger brother had died in a drink-driving accident a couple of years before and she was still having trouble coming to terms with it. She wanted me to go with her to visit his grave a few hundred miles away. As I held her sobbing in my arms in the graveyard, an icy feeling came over me.

'What if Joel dies?' I thought.

I imagined myself visiting his grave and then forced myself to stop thinking about it. 'Don't be morbid,' I told myself sternly. Little did I know that, by this point, Joel was already dead.

On the Tuesday night, he'd invited some friends round to my house for a party. By the time they arrived, he was already high on drugs and wanted more. They duly obliged and went out to score more drugs. At some point during the night, he'd started to feel faint and they'd put him to sleep in my bed. He must have died just a few short hours later. His so-called friends were scared stiff and just left him there for me to find.

I arrived home very early on Thursday morning – about five or so, after driving through the night to get home. Seeing Joel in bed, with the moonlight shining in on him, I smiled in relief.

I brushed my teeth quietly so as not to wake him and slid into bed with my head at his feet. The first sign that something wasn't right was the silence. Joel usually snored very loudly, but he wasn't making a sound. I got up and stared at his back for at least two minutes. Surely it was moving, I told myself.

Finally, my flatmate came in and flipped on the light. That's when I saw the vomit stain on the pillow.

'Joel! Wake up!' I cried out.

I tried to lift him, but he was stiff, his face flat and colourless. He was so cold I knew he was dead. But still I kept yelling, 'Joel! Wake up. Please wake up!'

As I gave his body a big tug, the air came out of it and it made a noise that sounded just like his voice. It sounded, to my tortured mind, like he was saying 'help me'. That sound haunted me for months.

Screaming, I ran out of the house. It was like I was caught up in a living nightmare. I saw his car outside and ran to it. It felt cold – just like him.

The next few days and weeks passed in a complete haze. I was in shock. I was messed up. I didn't want to live any more. It was all too painful. I felt like I'd lost a friend, a child, a brother and a lover all in one. I had a lot of trouble dealing with how Joel had died and whether he'd felt pain. I tortured myself over and over imagining what he'd gone through. Luckily, my family supported me but even so I found myself retreating into my own little world.

That's why, when Joel's birthday weekend came round in March 2004, my friends decided it was important for me to go out. Like I said, I didn't really want to go. But I knew I should.

After I'd got dressed to go out, I drove to the theatre where we were seeing the show. It was a really warm evening, very unusual for early March. When we came out of the show, no one really wanted to go home so I went in my friend Tricia's car to a friend's house where we all hung out on the porch, chatting and having fun.

I remember feeling glad I'd talked myself into going out and having this chance to enjoy the friends I have, instead of staying home mourning the one I'd lost.

It was gone two in the morning when Tricia and I drove back to the theatre where I'd left my car. Tricia had worked in a morgue for a while during the previous year and had seen Joel dead, which I thought might make things awkward. But in the end I found that knowledge strangely reassuring. We were feeling happy but tired and talking in that easy intimate way you do at the end of a long enjoyable night.

'I wasn't going to come out tonight, but I'm really glad I did,' I said.

What I meant was that there was some force pulling me out into the world that night, instead of staying home and going to sleep. At the same time as I was speaking, I had this sudden premonition that I wouldn't be driving back to my house in my car. I don't know why I thought that – it was as if I just knew it.

Right at that moment, another car, which turned out to be driven by a drunk driver, smashed into us. I don't remember any impact – just a kind of a sliding feeling. I was knocked out instantly. Amazingly, Tricia was unhurt. Later, I found out she looked over and saw me unconscious and was convinced I was dead. Given the fact that she'd seen so many dead bodies in her time as a mortician, I must have looked pretty bad. Poor Tricia panicked completely. Convinced that I was dead and that the car was about to blow up, she jumped out into the road.

Of course, I don't have any memories of this. My memories from the time after the crash are completely different.

The experience I'm about to describe didn't feel like a dream. It felt very real, although to begin with it was also very confusing and disorientating.

I was 'awake' but I wasn't in the car. I didn't feel like I had a body, just a viewing head that could look in directions. It felt like I was floating. I began seeing people, although none that I knew, and lights and what looked like a city. I seemed to know that it was Baltimore. Suddenly I was in a building and I could see someone sleeping on a grey and white couch. I knew it was my friend Pat. He wasn't talking to me, but I was staring at him asleep and thinking to myself, 'Oh, there is Pat,' and was extremely comforted by seeing someone familiar.

Although I stayed quiet, I was happy – relieved to be finally making sense of where I was.

After a while, Baltimore faded away, and everything was dark blueish-blackish and I was 'sinking' into it. It was unlike anything I had ever seen before and this is still the most vivid mental picture I have of the whole event. It was like water, but electric. Everything was dark and there were lines, which made me feel like I was under an ocean, yet there was no up or down, or sides. I think I could paint a picture of it, but describing how it felt is difficult. It is hard to find things to compare it to. It had no temperature. It had weight, when I tried to 'swim' back through it, but 'falling' into it was easy and relaxing.

Then I heard Joel's voice from behind my eyeballs; I couldn't see his body, or my body, only a presence. He said, 'Hey, Suzy' or 'Hello, Suzy' – I can't remember which, but he said my name and I felt really happy. I definitely said 'hey' in return. I was so excited to hear his voice. I felt like I was reaching to hug him, but then he said, 'Suzy, you have to go back.' And then, 'Go back, Suzy.' That's when the excitement of seeing him instantly evaporated. It's funny, given how much I'd missed him, but I didn't have any feeling like I wanted to stay there with him. I just knew he was right. I knew I had to go back.

Joel kept repeating my name, which caught my attention, and then he pointed or led me to where I should go to get back. Then he was gone – or rather *I* was gone. I very much felt it was I who left him not the other way round.

Immediately, the peaceful feeling that I had seeing Pat and talking to Joel was gone and was replaced by intense panic and urgency.

It was like I was trying to fight to the surface of this 'ocean' but kept feeling like I was drowning. There were what seemed like thousands of giant wheels or spheres in that 'ocean' and I wanted to catch one back but I did not know which direction to go in.

It was a really long, terrifying journey. I had a strong feeling of not knowing where I was. Or even where to go. It was the hardest thing I've ever had to do.

That was the first time it crossed my mind that I might be dead, or that this might be something to do with death. Until then, I hadn't really thought about it. Now, mixed with the panic at feeling like I was drowning was this fear of where I was.

Then there was a kind of whooshing noise – I'd say I felt it rather than heard it, but it was definitely there. When I opened my eyes, I was back in the car. It was the most amazing feeling, knowing I'd made it; I'd survived that journey. I was so happy.

Right from the start, I knew exactly where I was. I knew that I'd been in a car accident. I can't explain it – it was like I'd known my entire life that I was going to be in an accident at this very moment. But I didn't think too much about it. I was so happy to be back and out of that other world. I was at complete peace, and not panicking in the least.

Tricia, meanwhile, was running around the car yelling, 'The car is going to catch on fire.' Smoke was coming out of the airbags, but somehow I knew it was nothing to worry about.

I remember thinking, 'No, it isn't going to blow up, you idiot.' Which was a very weird thing to think because there was no way I could have known it wouldn't.

Then I looked up and there was a circle of fire-fighters above my head. They'd torn the roof off to get me out and I remember that it was raining.

A witness who saw the whole accident had called an

ambulance, and, once I'd been cut out of the car, Tricia travelled with me to the hospital. I remember I was still euphoric and very giggly. I hadn't had time to register any physical injuries yet and I was still so happy to be alive.

I told Tricia that I'd seen Pat and Joel. I remember feeling so happy about having talked to Joel. It was so tangible and vivid. Even talking about it now all these months later, it's still as real as if it just happened. I told Tricia about everything I had seen, about hearing Joel and seeing Pat asleep.

When I got to the hospital, I learned my right lung had collapsed. As I'm asthmatic, I have trouble breathing at the best of times, so having just one lung was a major problem.

There was also a scratch on my liver, and I had severe back pain. Doctors don't like to hear your back hurts after a car accident apparently. So they put me in a neck brace which is why the X-rays didn't pick up on the fact my right collarbone was broken until quite a while later. I was covered in cuts and bruises and in a lot of pain – but extremely lucky to be alive.

When I'd been in the hospital a day or two, my friend Kevin came to visit with the most bizarre piece of news. He said that, when he'd told everyone about the accident and about me being in hospital, Pat had freaked out. He'd started pacing around the room saying, 'That is so weird, I had a dream she died.'

I couldn't believe it when Kevin told me that. I was in total shock because Pat was the only identifiable person from my experience besides Joel's voice and presence. How was it possible that he'd dreamed about me being dead at the exact time I'd been fighting for my life?

Later, I asked Pat about his dream. He said that he'd dreamed he left work and went to my friend Stuart's house. He was surprised to find everyone sitting around the living room, not talking and looking sad.

'What's wrong,' he asked in the dream.

'Haven't you heard?' came the answer. 'Suzy died last night.'

For a while, Pat stayed there talking about me with them. Then he got a call and had to go back to work, and that was the end of his dream. It was bizarrely realistic in that it was probably exactly what would have happened if I really had died.

I think Pat was quite spooked about the dream when he heard what had really happened to me. He was caught completely off guard. 'That is really weird,' he kept saying.

I felt strange too, when I heard about it. And things were to get even stranger. On the day after the accident, Joel's birthday, his brother's wife gave birth to their first son whom they also named Joel. On the way out of the womb, he sustained a broken collarbone – his right one – just the same as me. I still find it difficult to get my head around the whole connection of Joel and his birthday, and his nephew being born on the same day, and his right collarbone being broken. I guess it will all take time to come to terms with.

The whole accident and the near-death experience has had a huge effect on my life. I guess I feel like I know something that others don't. Life is about experiences, and this is one of the biggest.

I still feel there was something pre-set about the accident. Of course, I didn't know I was going to be in a car crash, but I knew on some level that I was prepared for something to happen and prepared to cope with a long recovery. As soon as the accident had happened, I knew life would be hard while I was recovering, but at the same time I knew that everything would be okay.

I feel much calmer about death now. I don't want to die, but I don't have any fear about it. I know the spirit passes from the body.

I guess I don't have any pre-conceived notions of the afterlife – although my mother, who is a committed Christian, would be devastated to hear that. All I know from my experience is that there is peace in the dying process. I think there are many possibilities, but I don't worry about heaven or hell any more, although I was taught to. This is actually a great, great relief.

Since the accident, I'm able to pick up very easily on people's vulnerabilities – particularly about death. I can tell immediately those people who don't ever want to think about dying, and those who have made peace with the concept of death. I don't even have to talk to them about it – it's just something in the way they move.

I used to worry so much about whether Joel had struggled when he died. But knowing that I didn't feel any pain or have any fear, except when Joel told me to go back, makes me feel a lot better. I don't know if anyone told Joel to go back when he died. Perhaps he tried to come back and didn't make it. There again, if it was his time, then maybe no one tried to stop him.

I still miss Joel every day, and I miss having him in my life. But now I can grieve for him without being tormented by fears about how he died. I know he was with me during my experience following the accident – and I know he helped me in every way he could, and I'm really thankful to him for that. I also now believe that Joel had peace at the end, which makes his death easier to cope with.

Rest in peace, Joel. I know we'll meet again.

# 14

## LOUIS REA, 66
### MECHANIC, CANADA

MY GRAN HAD a dress that was navy blue with white rings on it. She used to wear it a lot. Whenever I remembered her after she'd died, which I did quite a lot, she was wearing that dress. And when I 'died', not long after her, it was that dress that she wore to greet me.

My grandmother was a huge influence on my life. My own mother died when I was two and I couldn't remember her at all, so my gran was the main female figure in my life when I was little. My dad remarried ten years after my mum died, but up until then my gran, and then an aunt, held my family together. Later, my older sister used to keep me in line but early on it was always my gran. Her death when I was nine years old left a huge gap.

The youngest of four children, growing up in Glasgow, I was expected to be quite tough and I certainly acted that way. Glasgow was a tough city where you had to learn to stand up for yourself.

It wasn't until much later in life that I became more sensitive to the feelings of others. As a kid, I got into a lot of scrapes. But, tough or not, I still really missed my gran when she died.

I particularly missed her when I reached the age of ten and became seriously ill with diphtheria. At that time, during the post-war period, lots of children caught diseases like that and, sadly, many of them died. I was rushed to the hospital where my fever raged out of control.

One night, the doctors summoned my father.

'Your son has a temperature of 105,' they told him. 'We don't expect him to last the night.'

My father, of course, was heartbroken, but, like many Scottish men of his time, he didn't really show his feelings. He had to be strong to bring up his four children and keep working at the same time. Certainly, he didn't make a great fuss and, lying there in a sweat on the bed, I wasn't aware of any particular drama. But then, I wasn't really aware of anything apart from the burning heat of my body.

That night, while I tossed and turned on my hospital bed with my father keeping a watchful vigil, my grandmother came back to me. She was wearing the navy-blue dress, with a dark-coloured cardigan over it, just as she had so many days when she was alive. With her was another woman who I didn't recognise. But somehow I knew she was someone special.

My gran and the other lady helped me up out of bed and stood on each side of me, my gran holding my right hand and her companion my left. I don't remember leaving my body or anything like that. I felt completely safe, not frightened at all, just curious about what was happening.

Together the three of us started moving along a long

corridor. We weren't exactly walking, more like floating. The corridor was dark, with doors going off to the left and right sides. But I wasn't interested in those doors. My whole attention was directed towards the light at the end of the corridor. It was the brightest light I'd ever seen. And yet somehow it didn't hurt to look directly at it. The light was so brilliant and yet, when I looked at my gran and the other lady, I could see them perfectly. The light didn't make them hard to look at or distort their features at all. I wasn't in the slightest bit overwhelmed by it, just excited at the thought of getting closer to it.

Then there came a voice. I never saw who was speaking or where they were standing, but it was a man's voice. He said, 'Take him back.'

That's all the voice said, nothing more. Then, all of a sudden, my grandmother and the other lady let go of my hands, and I was back in hospital lying in sheets that were soaked through with sweat.

'Dad, I've seen Gran,' I said excitedly when the nurses had finished changing my bedding and bathing me down.

My father was overjoyed to see me properly awake again, with my temperature back under control. But it wasn't in his temperament to make a scene or cry or carry on.

'You must have been dreaming,' he told me, when I'd explained about the corridor and the light and the special lady.

Yet I knew it hadn't been a dream. It was real. It's still real half a century later.

It wasn't until a few years had passed that my dad started quizzing me more fully about what had happened on that night. He was particularly interested in the woman who'd been with Gran.

'Tell me what she looked like?' he'd ask again and again. 'What colour was her hair? Her eyes?'

That's when I learned that the woman I'd seen that night was my mother. Later, he showed me photos that confirmed it.

Dad also told me that I'd nearly died that night because of the high temperature. The doctors had given up trying to control it and I had got incredibly weak. Even after that night, it had taken me a good few days in hospital and months at home before I got my strength back fully.

Looking back, I think that Dad was probably softer with me when I was growing up than with my brother or sisters. Whether that was because I was the youngest, or because he nearly lost me, I'm not sure.

I don't know what happened to me that night. I've never had another experience like it, and I don't talk to too many people about it in case they think I'm nuts, or else having them on.

I grew up to be a mechanic, and my wife and I went on to have a daughter who's now thirty-two. There's nothing in my life that has made me think I was singled out for any particular reason or sent back for any reason. I do get strange coincidences that happen, like I'll read about something I've never heard of before and all of a sudden I'm hearing about that one thing in loads of different places. But there's no big psychic plan. My wife and I are both Catholics but my near-death experience hasn't had any influence on my religious beliefs. It's completely separate.

The one thing it has done, though, is take away any fear I had of dying. I know there's nothing to be scared of. I think my gran and mum will be there for me again. And maybe my dad and brother who have both passed away since then. And who knows? Perhaps next time, I'll finally make it into the light.

# 15

## CHRIS RODGERS, 41
### SPECIALIST BUILDER, BUCKINGHAMSHIRE

SOMETIMES I'LL BE in the street and some stranger will come up to me. 'You all right, mate?' he'll ask. Then I'll realise that I've been standing there, staring into space for ten minutes, maybe twenty, in a complete trance. That's one of the legacies of my car crash – those blank patches where all thought empties out from my head.

I've lost big chunks of my memory too. Sometimes when I look back, there are great holes in my life where I can't remember where I was or what I was doing.

But there have also been other, less negative effects. Since the accident there have been various times when I've had a really strong 'message' about something, like a very powerful gut instinct, which, when I've acted on it, has saved me from a lot of trouble. Like when I was working in the finance business a few years back and I had this really, really strong premonition that I should sell up and get out – which I did – just before all the markets crashed.

It's weird. I'm forty-one now and yet my whole life seems to have been defined by a car crash that happened two decades ago. And the most bizarre thing is I came out of it practically unscathed, physically at least. I can't explain it. But then sometimes you just have to accept the inexplicable.

It was 28 May 1986 when it happened and I was driving into Bedford in my Lancia GT Turbot. I was twenty-two years old and full of the arrogance that comes with that age. As usual, I wasn't wearing a seatbelt. I never did like being told what to do, and this was my little rebellion. Also, I just hate that feeling of being restrained.

I'd just filled up with petrol and returned on to the main road when I had this really strange sensation. It's a cliché to talk about shivers running up your spine, but that's what it felt like. For some unknown reason, I found myself reaching for my seatbelt and buckling myself in. It was the strangest thing. But that one uncharacteristic impulse saved my life.

As I rounded a bend and entered on to a straight section of road, I saw a lorry up ahead in front of me. I was going really fast by this stage, probably about 80mph and decided to overtake the lorry. I had a clear view of the road ahead and there was nothing coming.

To my horror, just as I was overtaking, the lorry driver started to pull out himself, forcing me to swerve right out into the oncoming lane. I thought the driver would pull back in once he'd seen me but he didn't. Later, I found out that there was a little Bedford van on his left that I hadn't even seen, which he was overtaking himself. He couldn't have gone back in without hitting the van.

So there I was, going far too fast, and being forced across the oncoming lane. All of a sudden, my front wheel made contact with the opposite kerb and the car started to spin out of control. There was nothing I could do but watch helplessly as the car thudded into a ditch at the side of the verge and then, because of the speed I'd been doing, bounced out again into the road, where it continued to bounce from boot to bonnet and then back on to the boot again, before ending up upside down in the middle of the road with the roof all caved in. I landed with my neck bent round and my head pulled into the steering wheel.

I must have lost consciousness momentarily because I remember waking up in that eerie silence that follows a crash and seeing an orange and red blur. 'Oh my God, there's a fire,' I thought. But it was just the ignition light.

'Are you okay, mate?' came an unidentified voice from next to the car window. Later, I found out it belonged to the shell-shocked lorry driver. I couldn't move because of the seatbelt. The driver opened my door and leaned across to release the belt and I fell out into the road. After that, everything is blank.

My next conscious memory is of waking up in Bedford Hospital, with a nurse asking me whether I was all right.

'I can't feel my head or my legs,' I told her. Then I added, 'And what was that registrar bloke doing, fiddling around with my neck?'

From nowhere had come this memory of looking down on a room full of people in white coats standing around a table or a bed on which there was another person lying down. There were about four of these people and there was also a machine in the room. At one point one of the people in white coats was holding the head of the person lying on the bed, with their hands near the neck. That's when I realised that the person lying down was me! As I say, I had no conscious memory of seeing this at the time it was happening – rather, it came to me afterwards as a flashback while I was talking to the nurse.

She was looking at me, puzzled. 'How could you have seen that?' she asked suspiciously when I described the scene. 'You were completely unconscious.'

I couldn't answer because by this time I'd lapsed back into unconsciousness. Then, suddenly, I was aware of being awake again, but somehow detached from myself, like I was drifting around looking down on myself, although I didn't have any sense of being actually outside of my body.

Gradually, I became conscious of a light shining about 90 degrees to the left of me. I turned myself (although not moving in the usual way) to face the light head-on and saw that I was in a tunnel. It wasn't like a tube, just an enclosure of darkness with this light at the top.

Slowly I was drawn upwards towards this light, even though I wasn't conscious at all of having any bodily weight. I had a strong sense of being pulled, but I also felt as if I was floating. As I got closer and closer to the light at the top of the tunnel, I developed the impression that, once I got there, I'd pop my head up over the top and be able to see the whole picture, like popping up into a big globe and being able to see and understand everything.

But, as I approached the very top of the tunnel and could make out more of the scene within the light, I saw a bloke standing up there. Even from where I was in the tunnel, I could see he was leaning on a gate in front of a cottage. I didn't recognise the man. He was in his late sixties, I suppose, an archetypal old farmer type with longish wavy grey hair and a dog running around his feet. The man didn't speak until the moment I was about to pop my head out of the top of the tunnel, then he smiled at me. 'Are you sure you want to come in?' he asked.

I didn't see his mouth move, but I knew he was speaking and I could understand what he was saying.

To my surprise, I found myself answering 'no'. And that was it. I was back in the hospital, back in bed and momentarily awake. And yet, it hadn't felt like a dream. It had felt incredibly real.

This time when I went back to sleep, I didn't see the tunnel, but hundreds of thin lines, like ropes connecting people together. I had a sudden thought that I'd like to talk to my brother Steve, who was travelling in India at the time. In an instant, I was there, right next to his ear, saying, 'How are you, Steve?' Only I wasn't a physical person, more of a little ball of energy, hovering beside him. At that moment, I realised that I could go anywhere I wanted to – there were no limits. If I wanted to go to Australia, I'd be there instantaneously.

Then, once again, I was back in my hospital bed, waking up from a sleep. And yet, again, it hadn't felt like a dream. It had been real, as real as any experience I've had.

I stayed in hospital for two days. Incredibly, though I'd ripped all the ligaments around my neck, I hadn't broken any bones. The doctors couldn't believe anyone could have survived the kind of crash I'd had without snapping their neck. In fact, no one who saw the wreckage of my car – either on the road or later in the scrap yard – could believe I'd survived at all, let alone almost intact.

The lorry driver was probably more stunned than anyone – both about the crash and about what happened afterwards. He told nurses at the hospital that, after he got me out of the car, I'd wobbled to my feet and lurched off into the distance, banging on the first door I'd come across.

'There's been a terrible accident,' I told the astonished householder, before collapsing on their hall carpet.

But, despite my miracle escape, coming out of hospital wasn't the happy ending it might have been. I was wearing a neck brace but, even so, I was plagued with pain around my neck. I also had no feeling in my fingers and pins and needles in my toes.

I went to see a chiropractor who was taken aback by the extent of the damage to my neck. The day after my first appointment, I couldn't even get out of bed. Twenty years on, I still wake up every morning with a bad back and aching shoulders.

But worse than the physical niggles was the psychological fallout from the crash. I went back to work almost straight away – at that time I was still working in the finance sector. As my car had been totally wrecked, I borrowed my mum's car. About two weeks after the crash, I drove to Aylesbury, parked and went off to a work appointment. But when I'd finished I had absolutely no recollection of how I'd got there.

Panicking, I went to a phone box but found I couldn't remember a single number. Eventually, I got hold of a phone directory and looked up my parents' number (which, naturally, I've known off by heart since childhood).

'I'm in Aylesbury, Mum,' I said. 'But I don't know how I got here.'

Of course, Mum was really worried by that. So was I. Once she told me I'd driven, I had to trawl round all the public car parks until I found the car.

But, as I said before, it's not just lapses of memory that remind me I've been in a crash. I also have these strange flashes of intuition or instinct, even about the most trivial things. Like I'll be getting ready to leave the house and can't find the keys anywhere and a 'voice' will tell me, 'You've left them in the ashtray, you idiot', and sure enough that's where I find them. Or, when I'm doing a plumbing job (I'm in the building trade now), I'll get a message saying, 'Before you leave, why don't you just go back and recheck that joint you've just done.' And, when I do, there's a tiny leak that would have caused a load of problems if I'd just left it. It sounds crazy but it's as if someone's watching after me.

My NDE set me off in a completely different direction in life. I used to be arrogant and reckless and slightly dismissive of other people. Now I'm able to empathise much more with people. I can see both sides of a story rather than jumping straight in on one side or the other. I've lost interest in wanting to be in charge and in control. Now I think, 'Life just happens.' I don't get fussed about little things any more, like who's had to buy more rounds of drinks, but I do worry more about the state of the world and the future of humanity.

I still can't explain what happened to me on the day of my accident. I believe I experienced not death exactly, but a transition stage between the physical, earthbound, consciously aware state and a non-physical form where you still exist as a consciousness but you're not limited or linked to the physical world we all accept day to day.

I'm not scared of dying any more. My experience has rid me of any of those kinds of fears. The only thing that bothers me is about my purpose in being here – why was I allowed to come back?

I've had a lot of life-changing experiences since my accident

– I've got married and divorced, and discovered that I was adopted. But I've never had children of my own, and I don't know whether that was what my task could have been in coming back here.

I feel like I'm at a crossroads at the moment. I'm at a point in my life where I'm thinking, 'Okay, I've gone through all the nonsense. I'm ready for my purpose now. Bring it on.'

# 16

## JAMES ELDRIDGE, 26
### STUDENT, KENTUCKY, USA

I DIDN'T EXACTLY come from a house of luxury or anything. My mum and stepdad had five boys between them, so you can imagine what that was like. My dad (that's what I called my stepdad, as he was the only dad I knew) was good to us on the whole, but he was kind of a disciplinarian. Sometimes a little too much so. And my mum had come from a home life that was severely abusive on so many levels, so she didn't really have much experience of what a real home should be, although she tried her best.

We had a nice enough house, but hardly any furniture. For the longest time, we didn't even have a table. And food was pretty scarce. When we did eat, it tended to be the same old thing. Sauerkraut, sausage and black-eyed beans. Ugh, just thinking about them now can make me shiver.

Anyhow, given my background, it's not surprising that, when I fell ill, when I was still only around three years old, I wasn't diagnosed properly for a long time. At first, it was just a persistent sore throat, and feeling tired all the time. My mum took me to many of the doctors around our home in Kentucky, but no one really knew what was wrong with me. I think they kind of hoped it would just go away all by itself or I'd just grow out of it. Ours wasn't the kind of house where there was a lot of room for cosseting.

It wasn't until a year later when I was four that the doctors finally worked out what was wrong with me. For my mum it was the worst of all news. I had Hodgkins Lymphoma – cancer of the lymphatic system.

For the next two years, my life was a never-ending round of hospital visits and radical painful treatments. The really bizarre thing is that no one ever told me what was wrong with me. Being so young, I even forgot that I'd been ill in the first place and assumed that it was the treatments themselves that were making me feel so poorly. In hospital, I watched the children around me die, some with the same cancer I had, but never once did I consider myself 'sick'. Isn't that just the strangest thing?

My brother explained to me a couple of years ago that the reason they never told me what was wrong with me was because they didn't want me to think about it. They didn't want me thinking about dying, or asking questions about where I'd go. Even though my mum was a devout Christian for most of her life, I think they still had no idea what they'd tell me if I started questioning them about it. In all truth, I think they were scared, so it was easier for them just not to tell me anything. I had no knowledge of heaven or hell or an afterlife. Nothing.

By the time I was six, it was obvious none of the

treatments had worked. The cancer had then spread to every part of my body. I'd lost my right eye to it. It was literally eating me alive. I'd been put on all these experimental new treatments because, as the doctors saw it, I was going to die anyway, so I really had nothing to lose. But nothing worked. Their last-ditch attempt was to do an extreme exploratory operation, where they cut me open from hip to hip, took out all the organs and literally cut away at any tumours they could see. It was a futile gesture really – the lymph nodes are all over the body and they couldn't cut me open everywhere. I had a tumour the size of a softball in my neck and my body was backing everything up like sewage. In the end, the doctors threw up their hands.

'There's really nothing more we can do for this child,' they told my heartbroken mother. 'We're sorry but he probably won't survive more than a few more days.'

All the time I'd been in hospital, I'd stayed in cold colourless rooms with no carpets or home comforts – just a chair for visitors to sit on. I guess that's what hospitals are like. But, once they decided I was dying, I was put in a really nice homely room, with curtains and lamps. Even though I was still hooked up to a drip, the doctors felt there could be no further use for other medical intervention, so it managed to feel like someone's living room.

My mum stayed there with me for most of the time, although it was hard for her, having four other boys at home who needed her. In fact, she'd been by my side most of the last two years, trying to channel my sickness and pain into her, in an attempt to give me some release. The strange thing was that, occasionally, that worked and I'd feel momentary peace.

I hadn't been in the room long when I slipped into a coma. It must have seemed like the doctors were right, and this was the one sleep I would never wake up from. And yet, I was far from asleep.

At some point during that coma, I woke up to find myself on a ledge – a ledge that felt under my feet to be no more than a couple of inches wide. Not much footing to feel secure from falling. The place I was in was completely dark. I could see nothing, but still I could feel the vast emptiness. I couldn't remember my name, where I had come from, or how I had got there. All I knew for sure was what I kept repeating to myself over and over: 'Don't fall!'

I was extremely frightened at this stage. It was like, when you're faced with an extremely serious situation, like a car wreck, and your mind thinks so many things in one instant, just before the impact. My thoughts were jumbled: 'who am I, how did I get here, and don't fall'. I still felt like 'me', like I had a physical body. I could feel the bottom of my feet having contact with a ledge too skinny for them to stand on properly, and I could feel that my back and arms were touching some kind of wall. In that way, I could sense my body, but I couldn't actually see it.

While making a huge effort to keep myself pressed against this invisible black wall, with my feet on this invisible black ledge, I shuffled my way along the wall. I moved slowly, saying only to myself, 'Don't fall, don't fall, don't fall', and just kept shuffling. Since it was pitch black, I had no goal to work towards, or any sense of comfort. I was extremely fearful of falling into the abyss below. After I'd shuffled along the wall for an unknown amount of time, the ledge that I was walking on became wider. To my huge relief, it was eventually wide enough so that I could walk normally, no longer feeling like I could fall. I was now walking in the darkness, with nowhere to go, but no longer deathly afraid of falling.

'Where do I go now?' I asked myself.

That's when I saw a star in the distance. As there was nothing else around, I started to walk towards the star. The closer I got, the bigger and brighter it became. I started to feel more comfortable, more relaxed. As the fear disappeared, I grew more excited about getting close to the star and I started to walk faster.

As the star grew larger still, I began to see lines of light shooting out from it and to it simultaneously. Then the greenish-coloured lines began to lie down around me, creating a grid work, like that of a bitmap on a computer before a landscape is laid down over it.

I began walking faster still. The lines continued shooting out and began creating what seemed like hills and plains. But I wasn't paying much attention to the lines all around me, as I was so intent on the light ahead. My only goal was to get to the star.

Finally, I was there. As I reached the star, I saw out of my peripheral vision, what looked like endless rolling hills and grass. The landscape stretched on further than I could see, but I sensed it went on forever in its length. At the moment I saw this, I entered into the light.

This is where it gets difficult to explain, but I'll try. At the very moment I went inside the light, I also became the light. I felt like I knew everything. I knew the why of all whys, and felt everything that had ever or will ever exist to be one entity. The light was me, and I was the light. I was all, and all was me. See what I mean about it being hard to explain?

At this moment, I felt calm and peaceful, in the sense that there was no emotion. There was no sadness, no feeling of love, no feeling of hate, no feeling at all. I just 'was'.

I have to stress I saw nothing of significance while I was in the light. I saw no angels, I saw no Jesus, I saw no people or material objects. All I saw was light – and yet it felt that that was everything, just as the darkness had also been everything. I didn't need to see completed material forms. This was creation before it was created.

A voice then spoke to me, speaking to me through my voice, as if I was talking to myself. Yet it was also talking to me through the voice of every other thing. I was it, it was me.

The light told me, 'You have to go back.'

At the same time, it was like I was saying it to myself, 'I have to go back.'

To where, I understood. For why, I understood. I had no argument, no objection. All I knew was I had to go back. Nothing was explained to me because I already understood the reasons for everything. It was, as it seems now, purely logical and without room for doubt. I have to be here in the world, for the processes of life to take place. I have to be here to cause action, which causes an effect and sets in motion the things that have to happen.

After I left the light, I 'woke up'. I opened my one good eye and looked around. While I'd been in the light, it was like there was no time. It was only after I 'woke up' that I felt like it had only been a few seconds. The first thing I saw was my mother lying in bed next to me. She was fast asleep. I remember being happy at being in such a warm, comfortable room, with pictures and a carpet, after all the cold, sterile wards I'd been in up until then.

I put my hand out and shook my mum gently. 'I had to come back,' I told her.

To say she was shocked would be a huge understatement. I don't remember the exact words she said to me but I probably wouldn't have been able to understand them anyway because she was crying so much and almost hysterical at seeing me alive and talking.

She left quickly to go and find the doctors, before I had a chance to tell her what had happened. Then, because I was only six and because things happened so quickly, the experience kind of slipped to the back of my mind.

The doctors couldn't believe it when they came in to find me conscious and completely lucid. They were even more stunned when a series of tests showed that my cancer was in total remission. They called in a specialist who could only shrug and say it was a miracle. I'm not a medical man. I can't explain what happened. All I know is that I went into a coma riddled with cancer and, when I came out five days later, it was gone. I have screenings every two years but it has never returned. I think the doctors were kind of embarrassed about it in a way. I know they never really talked about what had happened. Every year there was a party for the kids who were in remission, a sort of celebration of survival and I went to a couple of those afterwards. You got a certificate and they asked how long you'd been in remission for, but I stopped going after a while. I don't know whether there's a limit on how many years you can go for.

The day I left hospital was one of the happiest I'd ever had. My mother had bought me some new clothes and even the fact that I promptly wet them (the medication I was on had a severe effect on my bladder control) couldn't put a dampener on the day, if you'll excuse the expression.

My NDE had a huge effect on my life after I returned home. I think the memory of being in the light and knowing how everything links together made it easier for me to put up with the years of trauma and humiliation that lay ahead once I'd left hospital. Kids can be cruel and the fact that I was this one-eyed boy who'd spent years in hospital made me an easy target for bullies.

Even now, as a 26-year-old adult, I believe that the way I think, the way I see, the way I hear has all been defined by my experience in the hospital. I've never forgotten how everything is connected, although this connection has always been so subtle. Sometimes I have had dreams about the future that end up coming true.

Like I had this dream where my house was full of people, just loads of people I didn't know. Now, I'm not the type to have strangers in my home, so this was unusual. In my dream, I was drifting around, really worried about all these people, thinking, 'Why are they in my house?' I remember specific details about them, like there was this one guy with really bad teeth, you know like a really bad mouth. And another guy had a really bad attitude. I didn't like him. I didn't want to be around him. About three months after the dream, I was meeting up with a girl I knew and it just kind of happened that she was meeting up with a group of her friends and they all ended up at my house. I didn't know any of her friends but, as each one turned up, I recognised them from the dream. They were all there – the guy with bad teeth, the guy with the terrible attitude. All of them.

190

In another dream, I was having a fight with this big Texan guy I didn't recognise. I punched him right in the face and I remember his face was soft like a pillow. A few weeks later, I met a girl from Texas. While I was round at her house, her brother turned up. He was this big fat guy. He got into a fight with his sister and hit her, so I kind of felt obliged to hit him back. It was just like in my dream; his face was soft like a pillow.

The thing about these dreams, as you've probably noticed, is that they don't really mean anything. There's no point to them, no deeper significance. Sometimes I wonder why I've been given this gift, if it's just to see things like that. Other times I think that maybe life is like a big circle and I've actually been round it a few times before and that's why I keep getting these kinds of premonitions.

It's frustrating because, when I was in the light, everything made sense and I understood everything, but once I came back all that knowledge disappeared and I can't find it again.

Another thing I can do is to read the emotions of others around me very easily, to the point at times that I'm reading their minds directly and getting direct impressions of what it is they want. I'm not saying I'm psychic but I've had many experiences that seemed psychic. In the end, these 'connections' with people around me just reinforce what I already know – that they are me and I am them. If I treat them well, then I'm treating myself well.

I've only met one other person who has told me they had an NDE – my stepbrother Todd. Strangely, Todd and I are practically the same age – he was born just one day before me. And, though he obviously had a different mum and dad to me, my mother considered us 'God-made twins'.

Anyhow, Todd tried to commit suicide in his late teens by hanging himself. Luckily, the rope he used broke, and he survived. He came to me and told me about it afterwards. Apparently, he'd seen riders on flaming motorcycles coming to get him.

'It scared the hell out of me,' he admitted.

Todd had been in a lot of trouble in various ways, and I believed maybe he'd seen a glimpse of something to come. I tried to explain to him that, wherever we go next, we take ourselves with us. So maybe there's a case for being the best selves we can. But I don't know whether Todd paid any attention to that – we lost contact about four years ago.

My own life is now at a kind of a crossroads. After working full-time since the age of sixteen, I was laid off earlier this year and I intend to have a break for a while and go to college. I haven't got a family of my own to support, so why not? I've always been kind of at odds with the way everyone else lives. My outlook has always been 'take life as it comes', whereas society seems to be yelling 'GO! GO! GO!' So I suppose going to college is a bit of a compromise between the two.

Sometimes I wonder why I was sent back from the light. I still have no real answer for that. Maybe it's just cause and effect. Maybe I have to be here on earth because of the role I have to play in someone else's life – maybe one day I'll stop something from happening, or cause something different to happen. Or maybe I'm just here simply to live. Because that's what light does – it creates life. It allows us to be here, simply to exist and enjoy existing. It lets us experience taste, touch – all the things you can't do when you're in the light.

I believe I'm here just to live my life, and everything that will happen will happen because it's supposed to happen. In the meantime, I just try to be good to people. I don't really talk a lot about this kind of stuff. I did tell my mum and stepdad and one of my brothers, but it's not the kind of thing people really talk about where I come from.

I don't know why I experienced what I did, and I don't know why my cancer was cleared. Maybe life can be partially manipulated by our minds. I know my mum never stopped believing I would live, and never stopped praying for me and encouraging other people to do the same.

I believe the light was the place of cleansing, and the place where the cancer was taken out of my body, but, without my mum's willpower and pure intent to have me survive, I don't believe I would be here. I myself had given up. I gave up on the pain, I gave up on my family. I simply gave up. I was tired, I was done. I was only six and I didn't know about dying, but I knew about sleeping. And I just wanted to sleep forever. I no longer cared for anyone or anything; I just wanted to be done with the pain.

In a small way, I think perhaps that's what made me so open to the experience I had. I'd reached a state of 'dis-want' for everything in my life, every single aspect. I suppose you'd say I had nothing to lose. Now, when I look back on the whole thing – the cancer and what came afterwards, I'd say it was worth having to go through all that pain and suffering, if that's what it takes to have the experience I had in the light. It has given me something in my life that very few people have and I feel really privileged.

People will read this story, and think their own thoughts, and interpret events in the way they want to. All I know is I went willingly into the light – and it changed my life.

# 17

## MICHELLE JACKSON, 39
### RECEPTIONIST, LEEDS

THINK OF A heart-attack victim. Bet you've got an image in your head of a fat middle-aged guy with a burger in one hand and a fag in the other. Well, you might want to think again. Because I'm thirty-nine years old, female, size 10 and a fervent anti-smoker. But, three years ago, I had a heart attack.

Looking back now, I hadn't been right for a few months before it happened. I'd been having occasional mild chest pains which I'd put down to indigestion. I was a single mum and working part-time in a dentist's surgery so I wasn't really living a very healthy lifestyle. I'd frequently skip meals altogether or else stuff down sandwiches while driving to or from work. Every time my chest would hurt I'd give myself a telling off and vow to start eating better, but of course I never did.

I'd also had a strange ache between my shoulder blades. It was usually worse in the mornings when I woke up and I'd put that down to carrying my daughter Leanne around all the time.

'You'll have to start walking properly,' I'd tell her, but when she held her little hands up and said, 'Carry!' I could never resist her.

I'd told my mum and dad about the shoulder ache and, as a special treat, they'd bought me a voucher to go and have a massage at our local gym. I was booked in for it on 14 May. How was I to know that by that day I'd be in hospital fighting for my life?

It happened on 12 May 2003. I was playing with Leanne, who was about two years old then. We used to play this game where she'd sit on the sofa and pretend to be in a boat while I crawled around on the floor pretending to be a crocodile or a shark trying to get her. A typically silly game you play to amuse small children. It was around 5.30 in the afternoon and Leanne had started to get crotchety like she did at that time, so I was trying to distract her while my mum was in the kitchen getting her tea ready.

Anyway, she was sitting there squealing and I was crawling around pretending to snap at her toes and fingers and stuff. Then all of a sudden I felt very clammy and sweaty and dizzy. I felt I was going to be sick and then came this massive pain in my chest, like Mike Tyson was crushing through my ribs or something. And that's the last thing I remember.

Apparently, my mum heard me scream out and rushed in to the living room to find me collapsed on the floor and Leanne still laughing her head off on the sofa, thinking this was all part of the act! Thank God my mum was there. I can't bear to think about what would have happened if I'd been on my own with Leanne. The doctors have told me I'd certainly have died and then the poor little thing would have been stuck on her own with my body for however long. It makes me go all cold thinking about it.

Mum called an ambulance and tried to revive me, but obviously she didn't know what had happened to me. She says now that, if I'd been my dad, she'd immediately have suspected a heart attack but, because I was her 36-year-old daughter, it never crossed her mind. She didn't think women even had heart attacks – mind you, I don't think I did either.

I was rushed to hospital near our home in Leeds. I vaguely remember being in the ambulance and someone saying something about giving me an injection. 'This might be painful,' they said but I didn't feel it.

Then the same voice was saying something about it not working and having to shock me. After that, everything is a blank again.

I've since been told that everything failed while I was in the ambulance and that there was no blood pressure or heartbeat for several minutes. In other words, I was clinically dead. The paramedics had to use a defibrillator to restart my heart and when I got to the hospital I was rushed straight into the operating theatre where surgeons worked for hours to open up an artery that had blocked the blood flow to my heart, causing the heart attack. They put two stents inside me to keep the artery open. It turned out that I had dangerously high cholesterol levels, something which is apparently genetic. When they tested my family afterwards, my dad and one of my brothers were found to be suffering from the same thing.

I was unconscious for twelve hours following the surgery. My mum, who'd followed the ambulance to the hospital with Leanne, was told that my situation was very serious. She now says she's so thankful that Leanne was with her, giving her something to occupy her mind, or she'd have gone to pieces.

Poor Mum. I feel really bad because, while she and the rest of my family, who arrived soon after, were worrying themselves sick, I was actually having the time of my life.

The first thing I remember after being in the ambulance was being on a long path. This path had steep banks on either side – it was kind of like a dry riverbed or canal-bed or something, but with no water. It was a lovely spring-like day and the banks on either side of the path were covered with grass and wild flowers. I felt really happy moving along that path, free of the pain of the heart attack. I didn't see any light up ahead or anything, but I had the strong feeling that I was moving towards something really great, somewhere I really wanted to go. I had that kind of thrill of anticipation you get when you're on your way to somewhere you're really looking forward to going.

As I moved along this path (I couldn't call it walking as I don't remember having any physical legs or feet), I kept passing people who were coming in the opposite direction. Some were people I recognised, like my ex-husband's father who'd died a few years beforehand. I'd always liked him and as I passed him we smiled at each other as if we were sharing some really great secret. Other people I didn't recognise, but they still seemed familiar to me and I was pleased to see them. It's really hard to describe how it felt, but imagine you're at a really fantastic party and you keep smiling at the other guests even the ones you don't know because you all feel so lucky to be there and you're so glad you've been invited.

I didn't worry at all about where I was or think about what it meant that I was there. I was just so pleased to be moving along this beautiful path towards this unknown but wonderful thing that was waiting at the end. At the same time I was moving, I knew in the back of my mind that if I didn't want to be on that path any more I could be anywhere in the world I wanted to be, that there was nothing stopping me going absolutely anywhere I wanted. But there wasn't anywhere else I wanted to be.

I saw a tree up ahead on the right bank of this path. I'm really bad on names of trees, but this was a lovely big tree and its leaves looked really green against the blue of the sky. There was a woman leaning against the tree. I didn't know her but again she looked familiar in a kind of reassuring way. I suppose it's like you might not know everyone in your home town, but there are some people you've seen around so often that when you catch sight of them you know you're on familiar ground. It was like that.

The woman was quite young – I'd say in her late twenties, and she had dark hair and dark clothing, although I couldn't say exactly what she was wearing. She was smiling at me in a really welcoming way. As I drew level with her, she called out, 'Are you going the right way?'

She said it in a really friendly way but as soon as she'd spoken, I got a really clear image of Leanne in my mind. It's funny, I hadn't thought of her at all as I was walking along that path even though in normal life she's never off my mind; in fact, my friends tell me I border on the obsessive in how much I think about her and talk about her.

Suddenly, as soon as the woman spoke to me, I could see Leanne's little face. I knew that, if I carried on going along the path, I'd be leaving her behind.

'No, I'm not.' I shouted out in a panic. And that was that. Immediately the path disappeared and the woman and the tree. I woke up in hospital surrounded by machinery. There was a woman sitting next to my bed and for one confused moment I thought it was the same woman I'd just seen, but then I realised that this one had fair hair and she was a nurse.

'It's okay, Michelle,' she was saying. 'You're okay.' When I finally focused properly on her, she smiled this really big smile. 'Your mum and dad are going to be so pleased to see you,' she told me.

Minutes later, my parents were there with me. They didn't stay long as I was still really weak and kept drifting in and out of consciousness but I could see from their faces how traumatic the past day or so had been for them. They had that shell-shocked look of people who've been through a nightmare and haven't slept.

I was kept in hospital for another three weeks after waking up while the doctors did loads of tests on me. That's when they found out about the familial hypercholesterolaemia. At least now we've been warned and my dad and brother can do everything they can to cut down their risk of having the same thing happen to them as happened to me.

I'll be on medication for the rest of my life and I have to go for regular check-ups. But it's a small price to pay for being able to see my daughter grow up. Leanne is now five and she's completely gorgeous. Of course, she doesn't remember the time Mummy went to hospital but she knows I've got something wrong with me. I'm just so thankful she hasn't got it as well.

I've told a few people about what happened when I was unconscious but they usually just say it must have been because of the drugs I was given in the ambulance or because there wasn't enough oxygen going to my brain. Nothing they say will ever change my mind about what I experienced. I know I was there on that path and I know I made the choice not to carry on going the way I was heading.

One day I'll tell Leanne about how Mummy came back for her, but at the moment I think she's too young to understand any of it.

Having a heart attack was the worst thing that ever happened to me but in some ways it was also the best. It made me really appreciate my family and my friends who were all fantastic while I was recovering and organised a round-the-clock rota to care for Leanne and look after me as well. And it made me rethink my priorities. Now I put my health above everything else. I make sure I eat really healthily − plenty of fish and vegetables and salad − and I pay attention to what my body's telling me. If I'm tired, I'll go to bed at the same time as Leanne, whereas before I'd have stayed up until midnight just doing all those things I couldn't do while she was awake, like ringing my friends and spending hours on the internet.

But most of all it has completely taken away any fear about death. I still worry slightly about the process of dying and, given the choice, I'd definitely opt for a less painful way to go, but I know there's nothing to be afraid of once you've got through it.

That's one of the reasons I've gone back to college. I'm taking a part-time counselling degree. One day I'd like to be a bereavement counsellor − I think there's a lot of comfort I could give people. It's funny, but, once you stop being afraid of death, life really opens up. The way I look at it now, everything is an adventure − and death is just one more.

# 18

## SALLY FIBER, 70
### CHARITY WORKER, MIDDLESEX

IN 2001 I DIED. That's something not many people can say!
Mind you, it was the worst experience of my life. I wouldn't
wish it on anyone else.

It started when I found a lump under my arm. I wasn't too
worried about it, but my GP referred me to a specialist at
Hillingdon Hospital to get it checked out. The surgeon I saw
was super. You now how sometimes you just take to people? I
really trusted him. I've suffered from MS for many years so I'm
wary of any kind of surgical procedure as I think it leaves me
slightly more susceptible to infection, but he told me, 'The only
way to be certain about this lump is to take it out altogether'.
He also reassured me it was a minor procedure – in fact if I
hadn't had MS I could have had it done as a day patient.

As it was, I stayed in the hospital overnight while the
operation was carried out. Of course, I didn't much relish the
thought of surgery, but I knew it was nothing to be worried
about so I tried not to think too much about it as I packed my

overnight bag. And really, there was nothing to it. My husband Arthur dropped me off in the evening and came to pick me up the next morning. It should have been so straightforward. But as soon as Arthur came into the ward the morning after surgery, he knew something wasn't quite right. I was incredibly sleepy and groggy. I could hardly keep my eyes open, even after he managed to get me back home.

After a few hours with no change in my condition, he phoned the hospital and was told, 'It's just the effects of the anaesthetic'. This was the same message we got later from the NHS Direct helpline.

In reality, however, I'd caught a flesh-eating bug during my 'minor' operation. Unbeknown to me, even at this point my kidneys were starting to fail.

Of course we didn't know that then, but by the following morning it was obvious something was very wrong. A friend came to see me and couldn't hide her concern at the state I was in. I could hardly keep my eyes open, my speech was slurring. My husband rang the hospital again. This time he phoned the ward I'd been on directly and luckily enough, managed to catch the surgeon who'd done my operation. I think that phone call saved my life.

'Bring her in straight away,' he said. When Arthur protested that they'd need to wait for an ambulance, the surgeon was insistent. 'No, come in NOW.' Incredibly, between my friend and my husband they managed to move me to the car still in the recliner chair I'd been in. Later I was told that if we'd waited for an ambulance, I'd almost certainly have died.

When we arrived at the hospital, the surgeon took one look at me and pronounced me 'very unwell'.

Straight away, I was admitted for a CT scan and tests and put on a drip to balance my fluids. The CT scan showed that though the kidneys were not damaged they were not functioning. There was also seemingly nothing wrong with the wound from the earlier operation. The doctors were mystified. It was only during a second scan a few hours later that one of the other surgeons on the team spotted a darkening growing patch on my right side. Necrotising Fasciitis was immediately diagnosed, the sixth case this hospital had ever seen. My flesh was literally being eaten up by this devastating infection.

The team knew they had to act straight away. They also knew it was going to be extremely nasty. The only way to get rid of NF is to remove the diseased flesh. Luckily for me, by this stage I was completely out of it and didn't have a clue what was going on, but poor Arthur knew exactly what was happening and was worried sick. He'd have been even more worried if he'd known what the odds were against me surviving this operation – afterwards my surgeon told me they'd been ninety-nine to one. In other words I had only a one per cent chance of pulling through. How lucky does that make me?

Mercifully, I don't remember any of the lead-up to the operation. I don't remember them giving me the anaesthetic or making sure I was unconscious. And of course I don't have any recollection of the grizzly details of the operation, the fact that the infection had spread so far they had to remove a third of my torso, from the top of my thigh upwards to my chest, leaving deep gaping wounds and my left breast literally hanging off. I remained unaware until later that the infection had come within a whisker of reaching my vital organs – which would of course have killed me. I have no memory of any of that, but in a way what I remember from the experience is far, far worse.

As I lay on the operating table with my vital organs shutting down and my body being eaten away, I physically 'died' as far as the medical staff were concerned. They miraculously managed to revive me. However, my mind was in another place altogether. The things I saw and felt in this 'other place' will stay with me all my life. Even though five years have passed, the memory of them is still as vivid and as upsetting as if it had just happened. Even talking about it now makes me tearful and distressed.

Suddenly I wasn't on the operating table any more, but inside my own body swirling around the different organs. I was in absolute agony. Each time I came to an organ the pain was excruciating. 'Why are they letting me suffer so much?' I kept screaming out.

I went on and on, floating around my body. As far as I could tell in this 'other state' I was in, the object of the operation I was having was to see what organs could be donated if I should die. Of course, this wasn't really the case, but in my 'mind' that's what was going on.

'I don't want to die. Oh, please let me go,' I pleaded to these unseen surgeons. 'I don't think I can stand much more.'

My wish was immediately granted. Just as a harsh, authoritative voice intoned, 'We can take the kidneys and the eyes,' I found myself away from the hospital and at the home of some friends. I was lying on a couch listening to two women having an argument about organ transplants and how they fit in with the ethics of the Judaism, which is my religion.

The older of the two women said, 'Under Jewish law you must not donate these organs.'

206

I then screamed out, just to stop them talking. I told them, 'My mother used to say something good has to come out of something bad. If I die I want to donate any part of me that can be used.'

Then I was back on the operating table where the pain was so intense I didn't know how I could bear it. Looking back now, it's so hard when people ask 'Was it real pain?' It's impossible to explain – I don't think I was 'awake' through my operation. I think the anaesthetic was working, and yet the pain was still undeniably real. I FELT it. I feel it still when I have flashbacks to that day.

Back in that 'other state', the surgeon announced through his white mask, 'Right, let's go.' Then I heard the crunch, crunch as he snipped out my kidneys. The pain was indescribable. 'Why don't they just let me go?' I sobbed. Then: 'No, I don't want to go. I don't want to die.'

Then, to my horror, the surgeon announced. 'Next it's the eyes.' Then he paused before adding, 'No, I think we will only take one, not both.'

With this I became mercifully awake and back in the 'real' world. To my intense relief, I could see. Yes, even though I was still convinced I only had one eye left, at least I could see. And I was alive!

Then, through the fog of the anaesthetic, I became vaguely aware of someone sobbing almost uncontrollably. It was a man and he was bending over me and sobbing. At first I thought it must have been my husband but when I thought about it properly I realised it must have been the surgeon, who by this time I'd got quite close to. It must have been a devastating operation to carry out, having to cut away so much of someone's body. I think he was just so upset at what he'd had to do to me. But though I wanted to comfort him, I couldn't move or respond. After that, thankfully everything went blank again and the nightmare ended.

Although, of course it wasn't really over. My first conscious memory when I came round fully from the anaesthetic was of being on a life support machine which was breathing for me. That was really unpleasant. It was horrible.

But that was nothing compared to seeing my wound for the first time. As I was lying down flat, all I saw was the nurse taking off a dressing to reveal just the patch on my thigh, around four inches by six inches. I thought, 'Oh, that's horrible!' But of course I'd been spared the sight of the main wound on my torso, where the surgeons had had to remove a third of my skin. Arthur wasn't so lucky and saw the whole thing. I don't know how he kept his cool, but I'll always be so grateful to him for not showing how he must have been feeling.

I remained in this state of ignorance for a few days. Every time the nurses changed the dressings they'd say encouraging things like 'Yes, you're doing so well,' or 'It's healing so nicely'. But then one day a specialist wound nurse came in to see me. When she took off the bandages, she actually recoiled. 'That is absolutely awful!' she spluttered.

That was really horrible. You'd think someone in that job would have been a bit more sensitive, wouldn't you? I think my husband almost hit her, he was so angry.

In fact, I didn't see the full extent of my injuries for weeks and weeks, which I think was probably a very good thing as it would have been a terrible shock to be confronted with the whole thing in one go. Of course it was awful, but you know, after the experience I'd had on the operating table, nothing could ever be quite that bad again.

I was in hospital for four months having skin grafts to try to cover the wounds on my body. It was a terrible time in so many ways, but there were surprising consolations. For example, my son had got married a few months before my operation and I got to know his new wife very well as she often came to visit me in the hospital. I'll always be grateful that we had that time together. It was wonderful.

My daughter had our new grandson while I was in hospital. My husband Arthur spent his time dashing up to see her, and then coming straight back to the hospital to show me the video footage he'd taken of the baby. He was just fantastic throughout the whole ordeal. It must have been so horrible to go through, but he was very brave about it all.

After four months I was able to come home, with the support of a rapid response team from the hospital, which has been fantastic. I was left with a wound around one quarter of an inch deep and seven inches wide that starts at the top of one thigh and winds up and around my upper body. It's still mottled from the skin grafts but it has healed up amazingly well. I'm lucky that, with clothes on, you wouldn't know that there was anything wrong with me.

There's still one wound left which has staples in it, and the doctors have tried to persuade me to get them removed, but I don't feel up to another surgical procedure right at the moment. I don't suppose I ever will.

It took me a long time to tell anyone what had happened to me on the operating table. I think I was still so traumatised by it, and so confused about what had actually gone on. I never asked any of the operating staff whether anyone had mentioned organ donation during my operation or whether there's any chance I could have been semi-conscious. And I never asked them why, if I was clinically dead as apparently I had been, my awareness of things was so incredibly vivid. I think I'd prefer not to know. I just want to forget all about it, but the problem is I'm still reliving it. It still comes back to me so vividly. Even after five years I can still feel the pain.

I didn't even tell Arthur about it until I started writing my experiences down in a book. I'll never forget how upset he was when he read about the operation and realised what I'd gone through. He couldn't believe all the terrible things that had gone through my mind.

But I wouldn't like anyone to think I dwell on all the negative things, because I don't at all. I view myself as incredibly lucky, really. I've had wonderful medical support and of course the help of my lovely family – Arthur, my two children and my five grandchildren.

Since coming so close to death, I feel so grateful for every moment I'm able to enjoy. It sounds like a cliché, but I really do seize every opportunity that comes my way. I feel like I've been given such a wonderful chance to have another go at life.

I know you might imagine I'd be obsessed by death after having come that near, but in fact I never think about it. Dying five years ago was a truly terrible experience, but it hasn't changed my views on death – it has just given me a whole new outlook on life.

# 19

# JOHN OWEN JONES, 39
## SHOPKEEPER, SOUTH WALES

SCROLLING DOWN THE computer screen, I weighed up
the various options on offer. I was after a cheap fortnight's
holiday for myself and my friend Martin — nothing too exotic,
mind, just somewhere we could get away from the drizzle of
South Wales and relax and enjoy a bit of sunshine.

I called up Martin. 'How does twelve days in Ibiza sound?' I
asked him.

'Sounds good to me,' he replied.

That was September 2005. I had no inkling as I punched in
my credit card details that this last-minute short-haul holiday
would be the start of the most incredible journey of my life.

The first few days of the holiday were pretty uneventful.
Martin and I got into a routine of going to the beach during the
day and then visiting a couple of bars or clubs in the evening.
We just had a few beers. I know Ibiza has this party reputation

but I've never been into drugs, I've never taken them. It's just not my thing at all.

On our fourth evening in Ibiza, we went out as usual, going round a few bars. In the second place we went to, we started speaking to some German girls.

'The barmen keep giving us free drinks,' one of them giggled. 'Here, you have some.'

She pushed her drink over to me. It tasted harmless, a bit like squash. I remember we all tried it, but it was me who ended up drinking most of it.

The girl who'd given me the drink was obviously very drunk, almost to the point of staggering.

'I can't understand why she's acting like that,' one of her friends said. 'We've all drunk the same amount.'

We know now that the drink the barmen gave the girls — most of which had been downed by this particular girl and myself — was spiked with a drug called GHB. It's known as the date-rape drug. Basically it acts as a massive sedative to slow the system right down so that the person taking it either passes out or becomes like a zombie, unable to put up any resistance to sexual assault. Later, the victims have no recollection of what happened to them. I've since read up a lot about the drug on the Internet and it's really frightening. Too much of it and you can end up with respiratory failure or else in a coma. Several people have died. And it's particularly dangerous when mixed with alcohol.

Later the girl who'd offered me the drink disappeared with the guys from behind the bar. Her friends were looking everywhere for her and when she came back a couple of hours later, she had no idea where she'd been.

Anyhow, I didn't start feeling any effects of the drug straight away. We went on to another bar and had a couple more beers. Then we met up with another guest from the same resort and went to his room to carry on talking and that's where the drug really kicked into my system.

The first weird thing I remember was almost as if there was a loop running in the conversation – the guy I was talking to would say something and do something and then I'd see exactly the same thing again, as if it was video recorded: stop, rewind, play.

That went on for a while and then I sat back and passed out, with my eyes wide open. Thinking back, I went into a kind of coma state. I just went.

Martin and the other guy I was with just saw me passing out but inside my head I went into a white room with lots of mist. It was as real as I'm talking now. I just couldn't make sense of it.

Straight away I thought 'I've died'. I wasn't scared, I was accepting of it. I thought: 'There you are, what's happened has happened.' I was convinced, 'Yeah, this is death'. Then I thought: 'So what's the next step. Come on, I'm ready.'

I've seen films where people see their lives flash before them in a kind of review and I thought: 'There's no point in that. I've cleared all my fears out through meditation I've done in the past. I've got no regrets, so we can skip that part.'

I don't know who I thought I was talking to. It must have been God or whoever.

I started asking, 'Who's going to come and get me then? Aren't I going to see any old friends, or family?'

But nothing at all happened. I stayed in the white room. So I started thinking that there must be something in my life left to review after all, some unfinished business. I thought 'I've got to review my life to get to the next level'. That's when I started to live out my whole life again. I know it sounds odd but I really lived it, in real time, although I know I was only unconscious a few minutes.

And it wasn't just the life I'd been leading up until now. I had lots of lives. I reviewed hundreds of lives and each death too. It took hundreds of years to live through them all but it was all in fast-forward right up until the end. I died hundreds of times, in every conceivable way. The ones I remember most of all are the violent deaths. I remember being a soldier and being tortured. I remember being stabbed. I remember being hung upside down from a wall with my insides hanging out. I remember being in the electric chair about to be put to death. And the odd thing was that throughout all these deaths the main emotion I felt was forgiveness. I forgave everybody. I felt all the pain of all these deaths, but running through them all was this acceptance.

After the last death I was back in the white room again and there were people all around. These were people who didn't play a big part in my life – people I'd walked past in the street in Ibiza. Then I understood. I understood that each person I came across was there to push me onto a different kind of path, that each stranger affected my life in some way. Like if there's someone coming towards you and you move over to the side to go around them, they're affecting your life. Perhaps something else would have happened to you if you'd stayed in on your original course. I understood that at any time, anyone can be a guide or a messenger in your life, even these strangers in the street.

I started shouting then. I was shouting 'What more do I need to understand?' Then images of absolutely everything flooded into my mind – the stars, everything in nature, everything. It was like being plugged into something and everything being pumped into your brain. It was too much.

Then I was back in the white room where I'd started and I realised I was dead or dying. I had a sudden realisation that if I went onto the next level, I'd actually be dead beyond the point of return. I started seeing beings of light in the upper corners of the room. I called them 'angels' to myself but they were really just white glittery things.

As I saw more and more of them, I felt like I was starting to lose myself and that's when I got scared. I said: 'Hang on a minute, I've changed my mind.' I decided I wanted to go back. I remember shouting out: 'I don't deserve to die here. I don't deserve it.'

That's when a thought sprung into my mind of my friend Martin. I thought, 'Well, if I'm here, where's he? Because if he's dead as well, he should be where I am'.

Logic told me that I couldn't really be completely dead and that my lifeline would be Martin. Sitting in that white room I started thinking about how I could get back to him. I was facing two opposing pulls – one to go back to Martin and one to go with the 'angels'.

What happened then is that I got angry. I took one deep breath and then I let out this almighty scream.

Apparently I really did scream. To Martin and this other guy it appeared I'd only been passed out for a minute then I started screaming. Later they told me it was spine-chilling. They'd never heard anyone scream like that. I told them, 'If you'd been where I was, knowing it was life or death, you'd have screamed like that too.'

Then Martin stood in front of me and said, 'John.'

At this stage I was still in the white room, but I heard him say 'John' really clearly. In my mind, I said to myself: 'Go to the voice, go to the voice'.

Martin's voice got louder as I got closer. Apparently I started doing that rapid eye movement thing at this stage. Then all of a sudden I was able to focus and look at Martin. All I saw was his eyes in among all this mist.

He said, 'John, look into my eyes. Don't look anywhere else other than into my eyes.' Then everything came into focus and I was back.

But though I was conscious, the drug was still affecting everything about how I behaved and I couldn't tell the others what had happened. Martin obviously wasn't affected by it the same way I was. I don't think he had as much of the drink as I had done and he didn't realise what I was going through.

It took all my strength to get back to my hotel room. That's when I passed out again. This time I was all alone. I couldn't breathe. I physically couldn't breathe. That was really scary. I knew if I stopped breathing I would die.

As soon as I stopped breathing I was back in the white room and I remember thinking: 'I am dead after all. All that stuff about passing out and waking up was a charade. This is real. I am dead.'

Then I thought again, 'But why am I still in this room? There must be something I have to review in my life before I can move on to the next level'. By this stage I really wanted to get out of that white room, but nothing I did made any difference. I was there for hours and days. I was desperate to leave. I thought 'Surely this can't be it?'

I lived my life once again, only this time I lived all the points where I'd come close to death either knowingly or unknowingly. I went back to those moments where, with a different turning or a different direction, I could have died. I remember being fourteen and passing out after getting drunk with friends in a field. I relived possible deaths I could have had that very night in Ibiza, like falling from the hotel balcony. I remembered having a 'magic eye' operation where they shove a tube down your throat with a camera on the end and I how I couldn't breathe.

The thing that really spun me out was remembering being born. Recently I was telling my mother about all of this and I told her that when I was reliving being born it was as if I couldn't breathe because there was some kind of fluid on my lungs and that afterwards it had felt as if someone had stuck something sharp down my throat.

She froze when I said that. She'd never told me before that when I was born the midwife had to stick a straw-like tube down my throat to clear my airways before she handed me to my mother.

There were a couple of dozen moments like that and then I was back in the white room. I don't know whether I had a physical body or not in that room, I didn't look. It was as if I was lying there paralysed.

I thought, 'Maybe there isn't anything more than this. Maybe this is death.' I just couldn't work out how to get out of this room.

I started trying to think logically. I thought to myself, 'If at any of these moments, I could have died, then maybe I can go back to them and pick up my life from those points.'

So I started to revisit my near-misses with death, but every time I went back I'd think, 'Yes I can pick up my life from here, but I don't want to'. The problem was that every time I went back to a near-death, I'd find myself having to live with the aftermath of that different path I could have taken. So if I'd nearly died after a fall, I'd find myself having to live in a wheelchair. Or if I'd nearly drowned on this holiday and they'd fished me out, I'd find myself lying in a hospital bed. I felt like a yo-yo. I'd go to these points and then think 'I don't want this' and I'd pull myself out into the limbo of the white room.

At one point I thought I'd go right back to the womb and be reborn again and live that life, but as I was following that path, I found I was once again losing all sense of myself, so again I pulled back.

Then I thought: 'If I have the choice to go back to all these points and can live them again, why can't I just choose to go back to the point where I've just left off?' The more I thought about it the more there didn't seem any reason why I couldn't. But as I started becoming my physical self again as I'd been just before I stopped breathing, so I was losing all memory of the experience I'd just had, which I didn't want to do, I pulled myself back into limbo. I said: 'I choose to go back but with memories of what's just happened.'

Then a voice I didn't recognise came from nowhere and said 'now's the time to put all that meditation training into action'.

I said to myself: 'Focus'. Then, 'I choose to go back'.'

That's when I became aware I was striking a deal with this voice. My part of the deal was that I had to share the knowledge I'd just been given. I'd get to keep the memory of the experience but I had to share it.

Even then, I kept getting sidetracked into other possible

points in my life, but I'd pull myself back and say 'no, I choose to go back to the point I was just at.'

Then I remember taking one big huge breath, like the first breath of a new-born baby and I opened my eyes and knew I was back. Apparently GHB stops your lungs from inflating, so that breath was a conscious effort to get myself back into the land of the living.

I had no idea how long I'd been unconscious. I felt okay but I was still having trouble breathing. However, I knew the worst was over. I lay there forcing myself to keep breathing, concentrating on each breath. It did cross my mind that maybe this too wasn't real, but just another part of death. But it didn't bother me. I just thought, 'Well, even if that's true, it's not a bad place to be.'

When I'd been conscious about an hour or so, my friend Martin came in. I said 'Where have you been?' He said, 'I'll tell you later'.

Once he said that, I realised I'd seen him say that exact same thing at least twenty times before when I was in the white room limbo. I'd lived this moment before. The realities seemed so blurred. I knew I felt like I was physically alive, but I didn't know if this was really pretending – just another type of death. Still, I reasoned: 'If I'm alive, I'm glad, and if I'm dead it's still pretty nice.' I still think that sometimes now, months on.

For the next four days, I didn't sleep at all. I don't know whether it was through fear or what. It's weird because the others who'd had some of the drink had the opposite problem and couldn't stop sleeping. Over the next days and hours, I pieced together enough information to realise I'd been drugged. A few of us, including the girls we'd met that night, had had weird experiences. Martin had been really sick as had a couple of the others. One of the other people at the resort worked in health and safety and came up to quiz me about what had happened. It was him who suggested it could have been this drug.

We went to the police and to the rep at our resort, but they didn't really want to know. It was like: 'Can you prove it?' Then they started questioning us about how much we'd drunk, as if it must have been our own faults. So we just left it.

Apparently it's a big problem. In Ibiza last year an Irish guy had his drink spiked with the same thing and died. It's a heavy sedative and when it combines with a lot of alcohol, your body can shut down.

When I got back I started telling people that I'd had my drink spiked, but mostly they couldn't really cope with hearing about the experience I'd had. I started to do a lot of research on the net and have discovered there have been around 800 reported cases of GHB spiking in this country alone.

I know some people reading this will think: 'That's just a drug-induced delusion.' I think there might have been an element of that when the loop-thing first started, but after that I know I really 'died' as a result of what the drug was doing to my respiratory system. Perhaps it's more that I was hovering between life and death.

Of course I was on my own in that hotel room, so there's no one to confirm that I really, physically died, but I know that's what happened and I know I made a choice to come back. I almost feel as if I cheated by using logic and willpower to say, 'If I have the choice to go back to relive all those moments, I also have this other choice as well – to come back to live in this life, at this point'.

The experience in Ibiza has changed a lot of things about the way I think. Now I appreciate people more, even people I don't really know. I understand that anyone who crosses your path can make a difference. Everything is there to help you on your way and you shouldn't ignore the signs. I know there's no such thing as coincidence. Just as co-workers are two workers working together for an outcome, so coincidence is just two incidents working together for an outcome.

I know that all through our lives, we're so near to death. When you're travelling in a car, just a few inches can make the difference between living and dying, and you might not even know it. All through life there are signs and pointers steering you onto a certain path, and away from death. Now I appreciate that much more.

I don't know whether everyone who dies or comes close to death will experience what I did. Maybe sometimes your body goes past the point when you can come back. There was certainly a point where I felt that if I'd gone any further I wouldn't have been able to come back, that there wouldn't have been any physical life left.

I'm certainly not scared of death any more. In fact I don't give a s**t about dying now. Before I was quite fearful of it. Now my will to live is very strong and I certainly don't want death to happen, but if it does I'm not scared. It'll be just like déjà-vu.

# 20

## KEN MULLENS, 68
### WRITER, QUEENSLAND, AUSTRALIA

YOU KNOW WHEN things are going so well it's like something is almost bound to go wrong? Well, that's exactly what happened to me.

For years I'd dreamed of taking time out from my everyday life and going somewhere different where I could relax and recharge my batteries in the sunshine and just see a different side to life. Finally I was living that dream. I was living on the Greek island of Rhodes with my long-term partner – and loving every minute of it. The days were long and easy, full of warmth and new experiences. I was having such a good time, I didn't want it to end. But of course it did. Brutally and suddenly.

Looking back, it's strange that I never sensed anything was about to happen because even from a youngster I'd always been extremely intuitive and had regularly received 'messages'. Well, not messages exactly, more like an awareness, of things that were going to happen. I'd know that someone – maybe a relative, or even a distant friend of a friend – was going to die in a certain way at a certain time. Sometimes I got bits the wrong way round, like I'd say the thirteenth and it would turn out to be the thiry-first, but usually I was right. I didn't really go round telling that many people though. At that time, and we're talking fifty years ago in quite a remote part of Australia, saying things like that would have got you labelled as 'mad'.

What I think now, after everything I've been through, is that we all have the ability to tune into these awarenesses, it's just that most of us have blocked it out. We're too afraid of dying and too consumed with our own needs to allow space for anything else. That's what I consider my mission to be – to convince other people not to be afraid of death. That's why I died fifteen years ago. And that's why I was brought back.

It was the early 1990s when I took my dream break to travel to Rhodes. I'd been thinking about taking time off from my career as music educationalist for years – both as a private teacher of piano and organ and as director of music at Trinity Grammar in Melbourne – to just relax and unwind. Though I loved my job, I'd wanted a complete break, which is exactly what this was.

It wasn't long, however, before a shadow fell across our Greek island idyll. I began to suffer chest pains and was diagnosed with a severe mitral valve problem. The mitral valve controls blood flowing into the chambers of the heart. Before I really knew what was happening, I was rushed to London for emergency open-heart surgery to replace my faulty valve at the Wellington Humana hospital in St John's Wood. The flight to Australia would have been too long and dangerous in my situation.

Of course it was all a shock. One moment you're living your dream and the next you're caught up in a nightmare with tubes and drips and hospital machinery. But I was philosophical about it all. I've always thought what's going to happen will happen, regardless how much you try to fight it. If someone says 'You're going now', there's nothing you can do about it. That's it. You just have to accept it. So be it.

When I was well enough to travel, we returned to Australia and to my home town of Mermaid Waters on the Gold Coast. I was on constant medication, and would be for the rest of my life, but doctors assured me that as long as I continued taking it the risk of heart attack was very low.

In time, life returned to a sort of normality, although I was obviously slightly more cautious than I had been before. I wasn't in pain but I could sense a sort of general deterioration. Then one gloriously sunny day in January 1991 when I was fifty-two, I was pottering around the garden when again I felt a constricting pain in my chest. It was like a slow closing down. I felt I couldn't breathe. This was accompanied almost immediately by massive vomiting of clear fluid.

I was rushed to hospital where I was told I'd had a heart attack. Luckily, they managed to stabilise me and the pain soon ebbed away. To help control the feelings of anxiety, I concentrated on breathing slowly and deeply and tried to embrace a meditative peace of mind. After that, I recovered well and was moved from the Cardiac Care Unit to a general ward.

I remained in this ward for several days, recuperating and getting to know the other patients and generally reflecting on how lucky I'd been. On day three I was walking around the ward as usual chatting to the other patients. But when I went into the bathroom, something strange happened. I heard once again the inner voice from my childhood, the 'awareness' that I'd received so many times before. This time it was warning me that it was my time. I was about to die. Again, I wasn't frightened. Life is what you take it for at each particular moment. You can't live in fear, you just live each second as it comes and don't try to change what can't be changed.

I went back to bed without telling anyone what I'd 'heard'. At lunch time, I was sitting up in bed tucking into a salad, when all of a sudden I felt odd, like something wasn't quite right. There was no pain, just an odd physical sensation, like a light bulb dimming and going out. I remember seeing a male nurse walking past my bed, and I called out to him.

'I feel really strange.' That is my last conscious memory.

The rest of what happened after that has been put together from my medical records and from talking to the medical staff. Apparently I'd had a cardiac arrest and doctors used a defibrillator in order to restore the heartbeat, but I kept 'coming and going' as they couldn't maintain the heartbeat. They worked on me ceaselessly for twenty minutes. But to no avail. Eventually I was declared 'dead' and the dispirited medical team started packing up the equipment. My medical records clearly show a graph print-out of my heart reading, which includes the 'flat line', the moment of death.

It's always a subdued mood when medical staff 'lose' a patient, particularly when they've been working so hard to save them. Voices in the room were muted and spirits low – until the sombre atmosphere was broken by a single cough. That cough came from me. The 'corpse' had come back to life.

Well, you can imagine the shock. Afterwards I went back and spoke to all the nurses and doctors about it. They said that when I revived I was still black and purple for a long while. It was the longest time they'd had someone 'gone' before being revived after a cardiac arrest.

So where had I gone? While my body lay growing stiff on the table, what had happened to the essence of what is me?

Well, I don't remember leaving my body and I don't recall seeing my body. I was aware of what was going on around me in the resuscitation room, of the people coming and going, but I could only feel it, not visualize it.

I didn't realise I was dead, but I realised something was different. However, I wasn't frightened at all. Instead I was excited. I felt extremely free and happy and interested in what was happening. I had a blissful realisation that, no matter what had happened to my body, I still remained aware, I still 'was'.

First I had the kind of feeling like when you wake up from sleep, but it really wasn't sleep. Then next thing I went into darkness - really, really black. There wasn't one speck of light.

I used to suffer from claustrophobia, but this darkness didn't upset me. It never felt threatening or frightening. It was peaceful, very, very peaceful. Then I felt movement, as if I was going somewhere, but I didn't know where. At some point – it's impossible to say when as time had no meaning – a light appeared which looked to be about a million miles away. I realised I was travelling towards this enormous light source.

It was like a hundred thousand suns – incredibly bright and powerful. And yet I could look directly in that light without any pain.

I could see what looked like clouds flying by, and I remember thinking, 'I'll put out my arms and see if I can touch them.' That was when I realised I had no arms. I looked down, and then realised I had no body either. I was excited to find I could 'see' in every direction at once. With my 360-degree vision I looked behind me and saw I had no back. I formed the impression that I was spherical in shape and probably the size of my physical head. Strangely, this realisation didn't frighten me; it was a feeling of 'oh well, so what'.

Time did not exist anymore. I knew I was still being drawn to the light but I wasn't sitting or standing up. I was just drifting in the form I was in, whatever form it was. At what speed I don't really know, but I know it was incredibly fast, like as fast as electricity. That speed factor was an important point; it was very, very quick.

But it wasn't just light. I 'knew' this was the supreme core or being, which I now interpret as being what I call 'the God-factor'. I felt drawn intimately to this supreme being which embraced me, and at that moment I was one with the light. Words can't really describe the magnitude of the all-consuming love I experienced while in the presence of the light. And not only love but perfection, peace, serenity, calmness and beauty. I felt that I was safely home. I was over-awed with the experience.

As I got nearer, I felt there was a form in the light that I could see. It was only vague but I felt humbled. I felt that this was something greater than great and I shouldn't have been there.

I couldn't see much more than what I imagined would be a head, but there were arms or what I felt to be arms in the light. They were outstretched and they raised me up. I felt ecstatic, but I still couldn't see into the form, I could look into the light, but I couldn't define that figure.

Then I was given a kind of 'show' of my life — past, present and future simultaneously. The easiest way to describe this is as if I was watching three reels of film at once, and absorbing each one individually but also all together. Of course in normal life, you'd only be able to take in one at a time, but I was aware of everything that was happening on all three. Even now, I can still replay it all, scene for scene, exactly as it was then.

There was absolutely no judgement during this 'show'. If anything, I was judging myself. And the most fascinating reel of all was the one showing what was to come. It showed me I was heading towards a more spiritual place. I felt really excited, as if I was preparing for a trip to a place I'd never been before.

Then the light, the God-factor 'told' me I had to go back. Actually it was more like mind language, because there was no such thing as speaking. I had a mission which was made very clear – to help people overcome their fear of death through writing books and talking to whoever would listen and whoever needed help. I was sad at the thought of leaving, but there was no question about it. I had to go back.

Then came the traumatic part. I can remember going back into my body, through the top of my head. Immediately I felt enclosed after the incredible freedom I'd just enjoyed. I felt hemmed in as if I was tied down or bound. It was excruciating. The experience had been just so powerful, so all-consuming that I had tremendous difficulty reconciling the free spirit I had just been with the cumbersome physical human form. I just didn't seem to fit – I'm not talking size – it just didn't seem right. I missed the freedom terribly. I still miss it now, but of course I've got used to living without it.

My first conscious memory after the attack is of being stroked on the arm by a nurse.

'Come on, Kenny, I know you can do it!' she was saying.

After that I was happy to tell anyone who would listen of

what happened. Some seemed understanding and accepting, whilst others seemed doubtful. The sister-in-charge was more than amazed that I was able to tell her, exactly, some details of what happened in the room with the nursing staff during my cardiac arrest, and even what she had been thinking at each moment. I accurately pinpointed exactly the moment she'd started thinking 'things are going wrong'.

'But you couldn't even have known I was there,' she told me, stunned. 'I arrived when you were already deep into the cardiac arrest and left before you 'came back."

I remained in hospital for a week afterwards, undergoing several tests. My overall prognosis was that I'd need regular tests and medication for the rest of my life.

From then on, my life changed completely. Although I was given only a slight chance of surviving the next twelve months, my partner and I decided to 'throw it all to the wind' and concentrate on enjoying each and every moment. I embarked on a world trip talking to friends, acquaintances and strangers about my experience. I also wrote two books about it which I have published myself. I want people to read them and know that there is nothing to fear in death and that something of us survives.

Since publishing the books *Returned from the Other Side* and *Visions from the Other Side* I've received thousands of letters and calls for help from people who've read them and who want reassurance that their loved ones are okay. Often I receive awarenesses that can put their minds at rest.

Although doctors didn't rate my chances of surviving into old age very highly, I'm still here. At times I really feel it's getting close to time and I'm excited – like a kid having a birthday party or about to go somewhere really exciting. I accept the idea of dying with open arms as just a path to another existence. But that doesn't mean I'm in any hurry to go. Believe me, I'll hang on to every breath. This wonderful and ever-changing world amazes me. Nature, in all her vastness, gives us so much to contemplate and revere.

It sounds bizarre but dying has given me life. I think I had to die to learn to live. It changed my whole outlook on life, my whole outlook on people and changed me from what I confess now was a bigoted type of person to being more broad minded and letting people accept what they want to accept.

Before my near death experience, I thought that Christianity was the 'correct' religion. Now, I feel there is room for all religions and beliefs, and sometimes I'm hesitant to even call myself a Christian. Sometimes I feel more Buddhist, sometimes more Hindu, sometimes more Zen. I hesitate to put too firm a label on anyone or anything these days. I suppose this is the biggest change in my life since the NDE – the way I feel less bound by rules and regulations regarding the whole spiritual (including religious) experience. And of course my psychic abilities and awarenesses have increased as I've come to have more understanding of them.

All in all, I feel like I was given a chance to go home, back to where I came from and where I'll end up again one day. But then I was sent back again to carry out this mission – to explain to people that, even in death, your mind, soul and spirit never cease. In the split second when the time of death comes, you will finally understand this. And embrace it.

# EPILOGUE

WHAT DO YOU do with a subject like NDE?

Rational thought informs us that it's an artificial construct, dually born from our misinterpretation of biological processes and our fundamental desire to believe that we are more than our bodily matter, that we exist beyond the corruptible edifice that is cells and bone and flesh and tissue.

The idea that death isn't the end but the beginning is a seductive concept, like a spiritual painkiller to dull that nagging voice inside us that says, 'Is this all there is?' Even its name sounds like a pharmaceutical drug, created in a chemistry lab to provide an escape from reality. MDMA, LSD, GHB – doesn't NDE fit right in?

And yet... and yet...

It has become human nature to believe that anything that glitters can't be gold. As if just the very act of glittering robs it of its preciousness. Anything that looks perfect must be flawed;

anything we really want must turn out to be unattainable or else, when attained, not worth the effort. So it is with NDE – because it's so appealing, because we want to believe it so much, we assume it must therefore be hollow and unreal. We created it out of our own desire and therefore it is illusory, insubstantial. To allow ourselves to believe in the possibility of another spiritual dimension is to go back to believing in Father Christmas – it's a lovely idea for a child, we say, but there comes a point when we must put aside childish things and face up to reality.

But, as we saw in the introduction to this book, scientific explanations haven't been able to fully explain away the NDE phenomenon. Certainly, we can find theories that rationalise some experiences but none that has satisfactorily explained them all. And to dismiss the very idea of NDE on the basis that the thing we most want must therefore be the thing we can't have, that we believe it because we want to believe it (which remains the logic of the sceptical majority), is to discount the experience of thousands if not millions of people all over the world who claim to have experienced a dimension outside of our own.

So far no explanation has accounted for the striking similarities in experiences that originate from such diverse geographical and physical circumstances. How do you explain that a police lieutenant from the American Midwest and a builder in Bedford, not to mention a doctor from 1930s London all report the same experience of being able to be anywhere they wished all in the same moment? Brian talks of realising he could visit the Eiffel Tower if he so desired; Chris took the opportunity to dash to Australia to visit his brother; and the anonymous physician could see things simultaneously 'in London and in Scotland, in fact wherever my attention was directed'.

Gabi in Hertfordshire and René in New Zealand could hardly be geographically further apart, yet both speak of their frustration at being 'sent back' knowing they have a mission to perform, and yet not understanding what on earth that might be.

Ninety-one-year-old Harry shares with 26-year-old James an experience of being at one with 'the light'. When Harry eventually made it to the light he'd been trying to reach, he describes how he himself became 'an integral part of that indescribable white light'. Years later, James, still a young child at the time of his NDE reports, 'At the very moment I went inside the light, I also became the light. '

Ken watched a review of his life, as did Harry and René and Brian, all commenting on the way they saw the good things and the bad things they'd done, but didn't feel judged for either.

Many of the people in this book found themselves facing some sort of choice about the progression of their NDE. Paul's mind was made up after seeing a vision of his grief-stricken parents at his funeral. Pat, who experienced hellish drug-induced nightmares during her long night's journey into day, vividly remembers the point at which she decided to live. Kate recalls happily falling through a kaleidoscope until the thought of her young daughter prompted her to try to struggle 'back'. The mothering instinct survives even death apparently, as Michelle also reports her daughter as being the inspiration for her deciding to step off the path that would have led, so she firmly believes, to the point of no return.

Suzy and Brian were met by recently deceased friends. Louis was greeted by his dead mother and grandmother. Jo stood in a beautiful park and chatted to a grandmother who was both recognisable as her own and yet infinitely more wise and compassionate. More than a quarter of the contributors to this book looked down on their own bodies. Paul was shocked to hear himself be described as 'dead'; Georgina was curious at seeing herself with her natural brown-coloured hair, rather than her habitually dyed blonde.

Common themes run through many of the accounts. Lines are mentioned again and again, linking people in some kind of invisible human grid. James sees greenish lines coming from the light 'like a bitmap on a computer', Janet's father talks about lines on his deathbed. Chris talks of seeing 'thin lines like ropes, connecting people together'.

Some of the people in this book saw tunnels; others saw lights. Some were scared; most were calm and content. Some asked to return; others were bitterly disappointed to find themselves back in the real world. Most would say their experience has made them more intuitively aware of what's happening inside other people's minds. Some, like Gabi and Sam, James and Harry even claim it has left them with some kind of pre-sight, so that they foresee events before they occur, a gift which is not always welcome. Some found God in the most general sense of the word, but most would hesitate to affix such a label.

None of the people in this book has anything to gain by telling their stories. Indeed, some would only do it anonymously and for others it was the first time they'd told more than a select few confidants.

Yes, perhaps they're all victims of some kind of mass hysteria that severe trauma brings on but, after talking to them at length,

I don't think so. Are they deluded? Are they just seeing what they want to see? Is it their brain chemistry playing tricks on them to produce this uniform set of symptoms out of a motley collection of circumstances?

So that just leaves the big question: Is what unites these people really the shared experience of having had their consciousness separated from their body, the spirit from the physical shell?

I don't know, is the cop-out answer to that. But what I do know is that there's enough doubt, enough anecdotal evidence, to justify a whole lot more research and scientific interest.

Every day in hospitals throughout the so-called civilised world people are dying in unnatural, often acutely undignified circumstances purely because of society's fear of death and our consequent insistence on prolonging life at any cost.

If the accounts in this book do anything, let it be to open a healthy debate on death and dying. It's easy to use the weighty cannon of science to shoot a hole through the fragile tissue of a few largely unsubstantiated first-person accounts but that won't comfort the millions who'll face death this year, or next.

What NDE offers is an alternative model to the 'death as a void' model that currently prevails. Can anyone really argue with that?

# BIBLIOGRAPHY

*The Journey Home* by Phillip Berman (Pocket Books)
*Life After Life* by Raymond Moody (Random House)
*The Last Crossing* by Gladys Osborne Leonard (Cassell PLC, a division of The Orion Publishing Group (London))
*On Life After Death* by Elisabeth Kubler-Ross (Celestial Arts)
*The Light At the End of the Tunnel* by Harry Hone (for a signed copy, write to: Harry Hone, PO Box 395, North Va 23128, USA)
*Returned from the Other Side* and *Visions from the Other Side* by Ken Mullens (available from his web site, http://kenmullens.tripod.com or email kenmullens@lycos.com)

# NDE ORGANISATIONS AND GROUPS

**www.nderf.org**

The Near Death Experience Research Foundation has hundreds of NDE accounts plus interesting facts, analysis, information and reviews.

**www.iands.org**

The International Association for Near-Death-Studies is a scholarly organisation promoting NDE research, education and support.

**www.horizon-research.co.uk**

Horizon Research is a resource centre for the study of mind, brain, consciousness and end-of-life issues. Headed by Dr Sam Parnia, it aims to provide information and up-to-the-minute research results on the central NDE question of whether consciousness can be separated from the body.

**www.near-death.com**

This website provides a comprehensive source of first-person accounts, religious interpretations, sceptical analysis plus a lively and informative newsletter. Webmaster Kevin Williams aims to turn it into the Grand Central Station of NDEs.